Self-Help for Women

The Ultimate Guide to Increasing Your Self-Esteem, Confidence and Assertiveness to Get More Out of Life

© Copyright 2020

All Rights Reserved. No part of this book may be reproduced in any form without permission in writing from the author. Reviewers may quote brief passages in reviews.

Disclaimer: No part of this publication may be reproduced or transmitted in any form or by any means, mechanical or electronic, including photocopying or recording, or by any information storage and retrieval system, or transmitted by email without permission in writing from the publisher.

While all attempts have been made to verify the information provided in this publication, neither the author nor the publisher assumes any responsibility for errors, omissions or contrary interpretations of the subject matter herein.

This book is for entertainment purposes only. The views expressed are those of the author alone, and should not be taken as expert instruction or commands. The reader is responsible for his or her own actions.

Adherence to all applicable laws and regulations, including international, federal, state and local laws governing professional licensing, business practices, advertising and all other aspects of doing business in the US, Canada, UK or any other jurisdiction is the sole responsibility of the purchaser or reader.

Neither the author nor the publisher assumes any responsibility or liability whatsoever on the behalf of the purchaser or reader of these materials. Any perceived slight of any individual or organization is purely unintentional.

Contents

PART 1: CONFIDENCE FOR WOMEN 1

INTRODUCTION 2

CHAPTER ONE: WHAT IS CONFIDENCE? 4
    WHAT DOES CONFIDENCE MEAN? 4
    BENEFITS OF BEING CONFIDENT 6

CHAPTER TWO: COMMON CONFIDENCE ISSUES IN WOMEN 9
    DISAPPROVAL FROM AUTHORITY FIGURES 9
    TRAUMATIC CHILDHOOD 10
    DEALING WITH ABUSE 11
    PERCEPTIONS ABOUT APPEARANCE 11
    CAREER TROUBLES 11
    NEGATIVE WORK ENVIRONMENT 12
    SIGNS OF LOW SELF-CONFIDENCE 12
    INABILITY TO ACCEPT COMPLIMENTS 13
    SOCIAL WITHDRAWAL 13
    NEGLECTING SELF-CARE 13
    ANXIETY AND EMOTIONAL TURBULENCE 13
    OTHER PEOPLE'S OPINIONS 14

- Shy Away from Challenges 14
- Worried About the Future 14
- Low Expectations 15
- Inability to Trust your Judgment 15
- Backing Away from Disagreements 15
- Constantly Checking your Phone 16
- Don't Speak Up 16
- Everything is Personal 16
- Blaming Others 17
- Constant Explanations 17
- Defensive Body Language 17
- Making Excuses 17
- Always Pessimistic 18
- Need for Approval 18
- Extremely Apologetic 18
- Pointless Lies 19
- No Boundaries 19
- Inability to Enjoy Success 19

CHAPTER THREE: PERSONAL BELIEFS AND WHO YOU REALLY ARE 21

- What Does a Belief Mean? 21
- Are All Beliefs True? 23
- Has a Specific Belief Worked Against You? 23
- Figure Out the Source 24
- An Alternate Meaning 25
- Eliminating Negative Beliefs 26

CHAPTER FOUR: SELF-DOUBT- SILENCING YOUR INNER CRITIC 28

- What is Self-Doubt? 28

- Overcoming Self-Doubt 30
- Being Real 31
- Stop It 31
- Stop Comparing 31
- Talk to Someone 32
- People Don't Care 32
- Journalizing 33
- Not Always About You 33
- Setbacks are Temporary 34

CHAPTER FIVE: 21 THINGS CONFIDENT WOMEN DON'T DO 35

CHAPTER SIX: 7 CONFIDENCE HACKS 42
- Hack #1: Act 'As If' 42
- Hack #2: Spruce Yourself Up 47
  - *Improving your appearance* 47

CHAPTER SEVEN: CONFIDENCE IN THE WORKPLACE 75

CHAPTER EIGHT: DATING CONFIDENCE HACKS 82

CHAPTER NINE: TAKING CARE OF YOURSELF 88

CHAPTER TEN: INFLUENTIAL WOMEN ON CONFIDENCE 95

CONCLUSION 98

RESOURCES 99

PART 2: SELF-ESTEEM FOR WOMEN 100

INTRODUCTION 101

CHAPTER ONE: SELF-ESTEEM PSYCHOLOGY 101 104
- Self-Esteem Includes the Following Elements 112

CHAPTER TWO: SELF-ESTEEM VERSUS SELF-CONFIDENCE 113
- Self-Confidence 114
- Self-Esteem 115

CHAPTER THREE: MEETING YOURSELF – IDENTIFYING WHO YOU REALLY ARE 120

    How the Brain Works 122

    The Two-Way Mirror 126

CHAPTER FOUR: SELF-DOUBT – SPOT IT, SILENCE IT! 130

    Self-Doubt is Self-Defeating 132

    Reframing 133

CHAPTER FIVE: FEARS, ANXIETIES AND INSECURITIES 136

    Measuring Up 139

CHAPTER SIX: 8 HABITS THAT BOOST SELF-ESTEEM 144

    Habit Number One – Dress for Self-Confidence 145

    Habit Number Two: Take It to The Tribe 147

    Habit Number Three: Asserting Who You Are 148

    Habit Number Four: Using Affirmations 151

    Habit Number Five: Adopt a Goddess Mindset 154

    Habit Number Six: Meditation 156

    How to Meditate 160

    Habit Number Seven: Do What You Love ANYWAY 163

    Habit Number Eight: Share your Story 165

CHAPTER SEVEN: WHY SELF-CARE IS IMPORTANT 168

CHAPTER EIGHT: SELF-LOVE – 4 PATHS TO SELF-LOVE 174

    Path One – Accepting the Now 175

    Path Two: Believing in What You Want Out of Your Life ... 175

    Path Three: Acceptance 176

    Path Four: Use Your Losses to Become Emotionally Stronger 177

CHAPTER NINE: SETTING GOALS 180

CONCLUSION 187

Part 1: Confidence for Women

How to Be Yourself in a Way Where Self-Love, Self-Esteem, Assertiveness, and Happiness is Your Natural State, and Self-Doubt, Stress, and Anxiety is Not

Introduction

Confidence might seem like an abstract concept, and there is no simple way to explain it. Some people might seem more confident than others, and you may wish to be more like them. Do you want to become more confident about yourself and the things you do? If yes, then this is the perfect book for you.

Most individuals tend to perceive confidence as believing in oneself, an idea, or someone else. Whenever a person displays confidence, they are, in fact, displaying their absolute faith in their talents, personal strengths, and abilities. When you feel confident, it tends to have a positive effect on your daily life, along with your ability to attain your goals. Confidence is directly associated with your self-esteem.

This book is the answer you have been looking for! In this book, you will learn about the meaning of confidence, general obstacles to confidence, understanding your personal beliefs, tackling self-doubt, and habits of a confident woman. Apart from this, you will also learn practical tips you can follow to improve your level of confidence.

Are you wondering, how is this book different from all the other self-help books present on the market today? For starters, all the advice given in this book is presented in an easy-to-understand manner. It contains proven methods and strategies along with expert advice you can use to improve your quality of life. As long as you are willing to make a conscious decision to follow the advice given in this book, you can see a positive change in your life.

These confidence tips are not just applicable to your personal life, but every aspect of your life. If you want to become more confident at your workplace, take control of yourself, and live the life you want, then look no further. This book has everything you need to become a truly confident woman. By following the simple yet practical advice given in this book, you can become more assertive, happy, and stress-free. This will allow you to get rid of any self-doubt and become a confident woman!

So, are you ready to learn more about all this? Are you ready to discover the secrets to becoming more confident? If yes, then what are you waiting for? Lets get started immediately!

Chapter One: What Is Confidence?

What Does Confidence Mean?

In simple terms, confidence is about having knowledge about your skills, abilities, and the value you provide. Not just this, it is also about behaving in a manner that conveys the same to others. Confidence differs greatly from low self-esteem or arrogance. Arrogance is the belief that you are better than others, whereas low self-esteem means you perceive yourself to be of less or no value. Confidence is personal, and it isn't the same for everyone. It tends to differ from one person to another. Different people have different levels of confidence. However, if you take a closer look, you will notice some signs that are common to all those who are confident, and it can give you a general idea of where their confidence comes from. If you're not a naturally confident person, then there is no harm in accepting this. There are ways in which you can build your level of confidence over time.

Do you ever wonder why some people are more confident than others? Confidence is a broad term. Defining it becomes a little tricky since it is so personal. Most individuals think of confidence as believing in oneself, an idea, or another person. Whenever someone displays confidence, they are displaying their faith in their talents, abilities, and personal strengths. When you feel confident, you have a positive attitude toward yourself and the world in general. No yardstick can be used to measure confidence. If you feel confident, then you probably are confident.

Self-confident people have certain qualities that others admire - it could be an orator who inspires others through his confidence and charisma or a doctor who is silently confident in his demeanor as he goes about his day. Self-confidence is extremely important in all aspects of your life. Low self-confidence is a common issue these days.

Self-confidence and success are closely related. Those who don't have self-confidence always find it difficult to achieve success. For instance, would you want to support a project pitched by an individual who keeps stumbling and fumbling for words? Well, you probably would not. On the other hand, had the same individual been loud, clear, confident, and had spoken assuredly and answered questions, the chances of considering his offer would have been high. A confident person can inspire confidence in others, and it is one reason why those with high levels of confidence are often successful in life.

If you worry that your self-confidence tends to waver, then stop worrying right now. Confidence is like a muscle; the more you train it, the stronger it gets. It is not a gift that people are born with, but it is a skill that is acquired. There are two ingredients to self-confidence, self-esteem, and self-efficacy.

Self-esteem is the way you cope with the happenings of your life and the acknowledgment of your inherent right to be happy. Your self-esteem might depend on the approval of others. However, most of your self-esteem stems from the fact that you have behaved virtuously and have the belief that you are competent at whatever you do. Whenever you work at improving yourself and achieve your goals, your self-esteem improves. It is the confidence you have in yourself that is required to be successful in life, and you need to be willing to make the effort required. It is a kind of confidence that prompts individuals to take up challenges and face life even when things don't seem to be going their way.

Benefits of Being Confident

Perhaps the two obvious benefits of being confident that you'll be more successful and happier in life. However, by digging a little deeper, you will realize there are more benefits you can enjoy by improving your levels of confidence. The more confident you are, the more you'll begin to value yourself and your abilities. It implies that you will feel more valuable and appreciated. When your level of self-esteem is high, you will be proud of yourself. You will naturally hold your head high and will not be worried about what others think.

For the reasons stated above, the more confident you are, the happier you will be with yourself. This makes it easier for you to enjoy the little joys of life without getting bogged down by worries.

When you doubt yourself constantly or question whether you can attain things in life, you are increasing your level of self-doubt. Self-doubt is the worst form of self-inflicted mental torture. If you are confident, then it becomes easier to avoid self-doubt.

The more confident you are, the better equipped you will be to deal with different situations in life. You will be able to learn, accept, handle, and even benefit from any circumstance you are faced with in life. Your mind will naturally tune itself to remove any fear and anxiety you might have previously encountered in a similar situation. When you are confident in yourself, you will be able to gauge any situation rationally without giving in to emotional responses.

When you start feeling more confident, you will feel more powerful and strong. You will become adept at tackling any problems that life throws at you. Whenever you are dealing with a testing circumstance, you will be able to face it bravely instead of feeling weak or defeated.

If you are secure about the way you perceive yourself, regardless of what others think of you, your social anxiety will reduce. You will no longer care about what others might think about the things you say or do. This, in turn, will make it easier for you to speak up and interact with others. Apart from this, you will also find the inner strength required to pitch your ideas and opinions without hesitation.

If you are confident and believe you can attain something, then you will naturally feel energized and motivated to work toward a goal. So, by improving your level of confidence, you can also improve your level of motivation to attain your goals.

As your confidence level increases, the amount of stress you experience will decrease. Apart from this, you will also feel like your life is comparatively less troublesome and free of unnecessary stress. So, if you want to be at peace with yourself and experience mental peace, developing your confidence is important.

When you are happy and confident, you will be more relaxed and comfortable - not just with yourself but with others around you as well. When this happens, conversations will flow more freely, and everything will be relaxing. So, your social interactions will not only become pleasant but even enjoyable. When you are at ease while talking with others, they will be more relaxed and at ease while talking to you.

When you are riddled with anxiety, fear, and stress all the time, you will not have any peace of mind. When you have peace of mind and are happier, then your ability to get a good night's rest will also improve. This will automatically improve your overall health. Confidence can make you healthy!

By now, you will have realized why confident people are more successful than those who have low levels of confidence. Now that you can clearly see the relationship between success and confidence, get to work immediately and develop those traits that will make you more confident.

Chapter Two: Common Confidence Issues in Women

Confidence is an important part of leading a happy life. Self-confidence enables you to believe in your abilities while maintaining a sense of competence in all aspects of your life. Low self-confidence tends to undermine your belief in your ability to stay competent and successful. Low confidence can also manifest itself in the form of inferiority, which can effectively prevent you from attaining any of your goals in life, or from growing. It is quite surprising that many people are not aware of their level of confidence or talents. Some might feel confident in one aspect of their lives and have extremely low self-confidence in some other aspect. Apart from this, many people also tend to have low self-confidence but are not aware of it, and this holds them back from attaining success in any form. In this section, lets analyze the most common causes of low self-confidence.

Disapproval from Authority Figures

A person's confidence can be severely impaired because of growing up with any disapproving authority figures. If you keep hearing that you are not good enough, you will believe that you are not good enough. This kind of negative self-image doesn't go away easily. We are all fond of approval. Approval is often the sign that others like what we are doing or saying. When a child is met with constant disapproval and harsh criticism, she will soon start believing that she has no redeeming qualities.

We all have an inner critic who keeps telling us we aren't good enough. With a little conscious effort, you can easily fix this negative self-talk. However, if your critic exists in your real-world and keeps telling you that you aren't good enough, you will eventually start believing this. If a child is met with harsh criticism, taunts, or disapproval, her self-confidence is bound to take a beating.

Traumatic Childhood

There are various reasons why your self-confidence isn't as high as it is for someone else. Childhood trauma is a common reason why children develop into nervous and anxiety-ridden adults. When not dealt with properly, it tends to have a lasting effect even in adulthood. Childhood determines and molds a person's life. Therefore, a turbulent or dysfunctional childhood can trigger feelings of inferiority and low self-esteem.

When a child doesn't get enough love and attention while growing up, she might start believing that she is not good enough and needs to change to get others to love her. Children from broken families or all those kids who grew up in households where there was constant fighting amongst the adults often blame themselves for everything that goes wrong. So, when the child grows up, she winds up being extremely apologetic, meek, timid, anxious, and riddled with inferiority.

Dealing with Abuse

Experiencing abuse in any form, whether it is physical, emotional, mental, or sexual can also lead to confidence issues. These kinds of traumatic events can make it quite difficult for a person to enjoy the world the way it is and trust themselves and other people. A combination of all these factors is quintessential to develop one's self-esteem. Even if one of these elements is missing, then personal self-confidence will be severely damaged. Abuse, coupled with trauma, can make any person feel emotionally empty. Apart from this, using any unhealthy strategies to cope with trauma can also harm one's self-confidence and self-perception.

Perceptions about Appearance

A common cause of low confidence is one's perception of appearance. All those people who find their appearance to be distasteful in some way or another struggle with confidence issues. A poor self-image is one of the main reasons they have low self-confidence. If they believe that others or society tends to look down upon their appearance for a specific reason, they usually shy away from social gatherings. Any perceptions about their flaws or even flawed perceptions about themselves are among the leading causes of a poor self-image. This self-image, when left unchecked, tends to have a severely negative effect on one's confidence.

Career Troubles

Perhaps you have a job that isn't in sync with the skills or abilities you possess. Maybe everyone at your place of work has more experience or is more qualified than you are. Maybe you have just joined a new place of work and don't think you can succeed. Perhaps you are overqualified for a job, and you feel it is beneath you. Being overqualified, underqualified, or having an inability to believe in oneself can all lead to a lack of self-confidence. You probably feel threatened by the way your co-workers behave or worry that you might end up losing your job. A combination of all these factors will certainly harm your self-confidence.

Negative Work Environment

If you have a bad relationship with superiors at your workplace, your self-confidence will take a beating. Apart from this, if you're surrounded by toxic co-workers, manipulative people, or anyone else who holds you back and doesn't allow you to excel, it will harm your self-confidence. Low confidence can also result from your inability to assert yourself. If others don't take you seriously or if others don't listen to your opinions, it has a cumulatively negative effect on your self-confidence. Since you spend a lot of your time at work, low self-confidence at work can easily trickle into other aspects of your life.

Signs of Low Self-Confidence

Perhaps you identify with one or more of the scenarios mentioned above. Are you worried that your low self-confidence might hinder your ability to grow in your personal and professional life? Well, before you can learn about developing your self-confidence, you need to understand the signs of low self-confidence.

Inability to Accept Compliments

How do you respond whenever someone compliments you? Do you say "Thank you" because you believe what they just said? Or do you try your best to deny the compliment or say something to downplay your achievements? Your inability to accept compliments is directly associated with your level of self-confidence.

Social Withdrawal

If you keep looking for excuses and reasons to get out of any social commitments or avoid making plans with people other than the ones who are absolutely necessary, it is a sign that you are low on confidence.

Neglecting Self-Care

If you don't take the time for self-care, it is also a sign of low self-confidence. If you think there is no point in taking care of your physical and mental wellbeing or don't pay attention to your physical appearance, it stems from a lack of self-confidence.

Anxiety and Emotional Turbulence

Whenever you are unsure of a situation or the potential outcome, it tends to cause anxiety. However, when you believe in yourself and have confidence in your skills, your anxiety and emotional turbulence will reduce. The lack of this self-belief is a cause for low self-confidence.

Other People's Opinions

Everyone is entitled to their opinion. If you keep worrying about what others think, you will not be able to live the life you want. If you spend a lot of time thinking about what others think or worry that others will not like you, it reflects poorly on your self-confidence. When you are confident, you will realize that your purpose of existence is not to make others happy. In fact, it is derived from living the kind of life that makes you happy.

Shy Away from Challenges

A confident person is not hesitant to take on any new challenges. In fact, they are proactive and will take on new responsibilities and challenges because they know it is desirable for their growth. If you avoid taking on any new responsibilities because you believe you will fail, it reflects your lack of self-confidence. You might probably believe that anything new is not worth your effort because you are already convinced that you will fail.

Worried About the Future

We all tend to worry about the future because we don't know what will happen. However, if you notice that you are always worried about the future, it might mean you have low self-confidence. This type of worry prevents you from enjoying your present and makes you extremely nervous whenever things don't come out as planned. A person with low self-confidence often believes that something or the other will go wrong and always waits for the ball to drop.

Low Expectations

Expectations might lead to disappointments, but not having any expectations is a sign of low self-confidence. If you believe that you will not be successful in life, or get much out of it, then you will stop trying. Accepting a mediocre way of life is not a positive sign. It almost seems like you have trained yourself to believe that some people are more successful because they are born with a special "something" that you lack.

Inability to Trust your Judgment

If you keep second-guessing yourself or are riddled with constant self-doubt, then it is because you don't have the confidence to trust your abilities. Maybe you don't believe you can make good decisions. If you constantly ask others for their opinions, it shows you are not secure with the decisions you make.

Backing Away from Disagreements

Disagreements are common. How do you react to any disagreements? Do you easily back out because you think you are wrong? In fact, you might even go to the extent of avoiding expressing your true feelings and opinions because of the fear of disagreement. Having a hard time speaking up or defending a specific view you share is a sign of low self-confidence.

Constantly Checking your Phone

You might keep relying on the phone as a means of getting out of any social situation. If you are at a social event or a social gathering, do you constantly check your phone? In fact, do you check your phone to the extent that you try to get away from conversations by doing this? If yes, then it is a sign of low self-confidence. You probably do this to feel like you're socially connected to make yourself look busy. The phone merely acts as a buffer, which prevents you from engaging in real conversations with others.

Don't Speak Up

If you keep second-guessing whatever you have to say or are plagued with self-doubt, then you will not be able to speak up during any group conversations. You might even hold yourself back, believing that whatever you say will sound silly. Since you're so afraid of what others will say or think, it becomes impossible to speak up. You might also believe that everyone in the group seems to be more knowledgeable than you feel and therefore hold your tongue. Apart from this, you might even wonder whether what you have to say is good enough to be shared.

Everything is Personal

A person with low self-confidence tends to take everything personally, especially criticism. Well, if you want to grow in life, you will need to deal with criticism. Your inability to stomach criticism or take it positively is a sign that you don't believe in yourself. If you react emotionally or become extremely defensive, it is a sign of low self-confidence.

Blaming Others

Constantly blaming others when things don't turn out like they were supposed to, is a sign of low self-confidence. The inability to shoulder any responsibility regardless of the outcome by shifting the blame onto others is a negative trait. Apart from this, if you notice that you constantly complain, then you might be suffering from low self-confidence. This is a common strategy where people assume the role of a victim who has little or no control over the happenings in their life.

Constant Explanations

Do you feel a constant need to keep explaining your actions, thoughts, or opinions? Everyone makes mistakes, but a person with low self-confidence often feels the need to justify their decisions, even if they are right.

Defensive Body Language

Using defensive body language, like stern facial expressions, or crossing your arms is a sign that you do not want to allow anyone else in and are trying to shut people out. By physically closing off your body language, it shows you are uncomfortable or anxious in the present circumstances.

Making Excuses

A person with low self-confidence often makes excuses to define their actions and choices, especially when criticized, so they don't seem inferior. To such people, accepting any form of personal responsibility feels like a sign of weakness. Well, accepting personal responsibility is a sign of inner strength and awareness. A person with low self-confidence fails to understand this. A confident person stops and listens to criticism without getting defensive. They can give a context to any criticism they receive.

Always Pessimistic

If you notice that you are always pessimistic or extremely critical of everything that happens, then it is a sign of low self-confidence. All the negative beliefs that are present within you tend to come out in the form of negative feelings. This kind of pessimism is the result of the feeling that you have no control over your own life.

Need for Approval

A confident person knows not to depend on external sources of approval to feel better. A person with low self-confidence, on the other hand, seeks constant validation and approval from others to feel better about herself. Not getting the approval that you need can also be a cause of frustration. A person with confidence issues is unable to understand the simple fact that not everyone will approve of her.

Extremely Apologetic

Apologizing shows you can understand when you make mistakes. However, constant apologies show that you don't trust yourself. Only apologize when you go wrong or hurt someone else. People with low self-confidence are incapable of understanding their true self-worth. It prompts them to believe that everything they do is wrong, which makes them apologize.

Pointless Lies

A person with low self-confidence believes that the truth is not interesting. To make themselves seem more interesting, they tend to invent pointless white lies. If you don't feel like sharing the truth because you are worried about how others will perceive you, it is a sign of low self-confidence. If you tell white lies because you want others to think highly of you, it shows you don't love yourself.

No Boundaries

A person dealing with self-confidence issues might not be comfortable to draw and maintain personal boundaries. Establishing boundaries shows you love and care for yourself. Since you are worried about how others will perceive you, you always crave for the positive feedback. By establishing boundaries, you might not get this kind of feedback.

Inability to Enjoy Success

If you notice that you downplay your achievements or cannot enjoy your success, it is a sign of low self-confidence. If you associate your success with luck instead of the skills you possess, it is not a good sign.

Now that you have gone through the list of different kinds of low self-confidence, check off all those points you agree with. This simple exercise will help you gauge your level of self-confidence and make you aware of your behaviors, which will help you in your journey of building confidence.

Chapter Three: Personal Beliefs and Who You Really Are

What Does a Belief Mean?

A belief is a mental notion or assumption you have about yourself as well as the world in general. The thing with beliefs is that the mind tends to think these beliefs are absolute truths. Our beliefs can be tied to us emotionally and psychologically and are often irrational at the core. All the beliefs you have are a culmination of all the previous experiences and interactions you had with the world. This includes both good and bad experiences. Essentially, a belief defines your mental make-up.

Beliefs serve as a guide for our subconscious mind to function on autopilot. Once they are formed, they are deeply ingrained within us. We tend to take them for granted and believe them to be facts, regardless of whether they are true.

These beliefs firmly stick in our minds and can hinder our growth, especially when they are wrong. A negative belief can hold you back and does not allow you to capitalize on your full potential. Most of the beliefs you hold as an adult result from various childhood experiences. You might have picked up these beliefs from other people as well. For instance, whenever a child does something wrong, the parent might scold or criticize him for what the child did. As a result of this, the child might begin to believe that they are not good enough. This belief will influence any or all other existing and newly gained beliefs the child carries with him into adulthood.

There are two ways in which we form beliefs. Beliefs are either based on your experiences or inferences. Beliefs can also be based on things that others say, especially when you have accepted them to be the truth.

All the beliefs that are associated with relationships tend to be deeply rooted since these events are extremely emotional and have a lasting impact on one's subconscious mind. For instance, dealing with a nasty breakup might influence the way you perceive yourself. You might even start believing you are incapable of being loved or loving anyone else. Beliefs of this sort are negative and highly undesirable. Grab a sheet of paper and make a note of some beliefs you might have formed in your mind and have accepted to be the absolute truth.

You probably don't accept these beliefs on a conscious level but tend to react to them emotionally. Some instances of a few common and undesirable beliefs include the following:

- I am not good enough and will never be good enough.
- I haven't managed to achieve anything in life and will go nowhere.
- I am not smart enough, and that's why people don't take me seriously.
- I'm not capable of being loved, and I will never find true love.

Apart from these obvious beliefs, other common negative beliefs include thoughts such as, "I am too old, I am too young, I am not good looking, I am unlucky, I am useless," and so on. The list is endless. Start making a note of all the beliefs you have, and once you do this, you can become more aware of the beliefs that you hold.

Are All Beliefs True?

The next step is to understand whether your beliefs are true. Just because you believe in something doesn't mean that it is the absolute truth. Now that you're aware of all the negative beliefs you have in your mind, pick one of these beliefs and check whether or not it is the truth. For instance, if you think you are a bad writer, go down your memory lane and think of one article, letter, or anything you have written that others praised. If you believe that you are not good looking, then think of a time when someone complimented you. If you think you are not smart enough, then think of situations in your life you thought were impossible, yet you overcame them. This step is quite important because it allows you to understand that your beliefs are not necessarily true. You can go through your day thinking of all the things that contradict your beliefs. If you can contradict a specific belief, then let us move onto the next step.

Has a Specific Belief Worked Against You?

Think of all the different instances in your life where a specific belief worked against you. Perhaps it kept you away from doing something you always wanted to do or affected your overall personality negatively. It might have hurt your relationships, your state of mind, and even your general attitude or perception toward life. Think of all these instances and start writing them down. If you want to change something, then you need to take charge of the situation and do something about it. I believe pain to be an accelerant for change. When all your experiences have been a disappointment, then your willingness to change your life and shake things up a bit will increase. Now, you need to close your eyes and think back to all the painful moments and then visualize them. Make this visualization as real as possible and allow yourself to experience the pain all over again. You cannot change unless you really want to change. By visualizing these painful incidents, your willingness to change will increase.

Figure Out the Source

This step requires you to think a little deeper and go back to the memories of your past, preferably your childhood or teenage years. Now that you visualize an event that caused you pain, think about all the instances that led to this event. Think of the triggers and other factors that led to you feeling pain. Once you figure all this out, start writing them down and give yourself a detailed description of the event. When you close your eyes and start thinking about all the factors that led to a specific incident, it will even trigger emotions associated with a specific instance stored in your subconscious.

For instance, if you believe you are not good enough, then think of all the different reasons that led to this belief in your subconscious. It could be the comments made by others during your childhood. Another reason could be any disappointment expressed by authority figures in your life whenever you didn't behave in a manner that they expected. It could also be because of peer pressure you might have endured during early childhood and teenage years. Once you have identified the source, try to visualize that specific scenario and make it as detailed as possible.

An Alternate Meaning

The event you have identified in the previous step might not necessarily be the only reason for the negative beliefs you have formed. In fact, it might not even be fully true. Just because someone in your high school thought the essay you had written wasn't good enough doesn't mean you are a bad writer. You might have believed a specific belief because you thought it was the irrefutable truth. In reality, it just means you adopted a specific perspective that was negative and went ahead with it. You didn't even test any other alternative yet plausible explanations for a specific situation your belief stems from.

A particular situation can have different meanings apart from the one that you have attached to it. The event influences you because you allowed it to influence you. Now, think of all the reasonable alternatives you can think of for a specific situation. You might be able to come up with alternate meanings when you think about it from the perspective of a neutral party. Go back to the instance when you thought you were a bad writer; there was likely some other plausible explanation. Perhaps the teacher was having a bad day, or maybe your style of writing differed from that which the teacher expected. Perhaps it was just nervousness.

Similarly, if you think you're not good enough, then think of the alternate reasons why your parents might have reacted harshly. Perhaps they were upset about something else, and when they said you are not good enough, it was just a single moment of anger. Now, try to visualize this same situation, but allow your newly gained alternate explanations to influence the way you feel about it. Once you do this, you will realize that you have the power to lend meaning to any situation. If you think you are not good enough, then it is because you have allowed yourself to believe you're not good enough.

Eliminating Negative Beliefs

Here are three simple steps you can practice in order to remove many negative beliefs from your mind.

The first step is to close your eyes and visualize a scenario that has contributed toward forming the negative beliefs. Now, imagine that this scene is slowly fading away until it becomes hazy and distant. It almost feels like someone has turned out the lights, and you are still trying to see. Now, visualize the scene slowly moving away. As the scene starts pulling away from your mind, allow it to become blurry. Keep doing this until it becomes nothing more than a distant memory and it shrinks into nothingness. You will be left with darkness. Now, breathe in slowly and breathe out slowly. Take a couple of deep breaths and allow your mind to calm down.

In the second step, slowly open your eyes and write down a statement that contradicts a specific belief you have. For instance, if you believe you are a bad writer, or you are not good enough, make a note that you are a good writer and you are a very warm and loving person. This step requires you to write something that isn't consistent with the beliefs you already have in your mind.

The third step is to remove the negative beliefs from your visualization. Close your eyes. Try to visualize how you would feel if the statement you had written in the previous step was true. Visualize that you are a good writer and are working on a book on your laptop in an elegantly furnished office. Perhaps you can visualize yourself walking in a lush green meadow on a sunny morning, knowing fully that you are a wonderful person. Think about all the different details in this scene. What are the different things that you can see in this visualization? Are there any specific sights or smells you can experience? Are there things in your visualization that you can touch? Think about all these things and allow yourself to feel every emotion with no judgment. Once you do this, you might end up smiling. Now, try to make your visualization a little brighter as if someone has turned the spotlight on your visualization. When you go through all the steps, evaluate how you feel and think if the situation still bothers you.

Your actions and beliefs are closely related. If the way you act is not in sync with your beliefs, then those beliefs will slowly fade away and lose their credibility. It essentially paves the way for a new set of beliefs that are validated by signals generated by your new behaviors. It might sound a little complicated, but it is quite simple. It all boils down to the way you talk to yourself and think. If you start talking and behaving like a confident person, your confidence levels will increase. When you start feeling confident, your perception changes, and from this perception, new beliefs are formed. Motivation is also closely associated with confidence. Therefore, the more confident you are, the more motivated you will be in life.

Most of us tend to forget that we are the creators of our own beliefs and that we are the only ones who have the power to change our beliefs. Keep in mind that there is more to a situation than the way you interpret it. Just because you think something is true doesn't necessarily mean it is true. You have the power to change your perspective, and only when you change your perspective will you be able to change your beliefs.

If you are keen on changing your limiting beliefs, then start using the different tips given in this chapter. All that you need to do is carefully read through the steps discussed, grab a paper and pen, find a quiet spot for yourself, and start writing your thoughts. It will give you a better understanding of your beliefs and how to change them.

Chapter Four: Self-Doubt- Silencing Your Inner Critic

What is Self-Doubt?

Experiencing self-doubt is all too common, and most of us will have experienced it at one point or another. However, what matters is the way you deal with it, how you cope with it, and what you do with it. It makes all the difference between chronically struggling with self-doubt and allowing it to pass you by. If you keep regularly experiencing self-doubt, you might ask yourself, why does everyone else seem to do well when I'm struggling?

To a certain extent, self-doubt is healthy. Self-doubt enables you to understand when you're not doing something right. With self-doubt, you tend to question and challenge yourself, which prompts internal inquiry. Self-doubt can also bring about humility and increase your understanding of others.

The society we live in values the extraordinary. Therefore, it is common for self-doubt to become a chronic state instead of a fleeting one. When it becomes chronic, you often stand in your own way, and it leads to self-sabotaging thoughts. Even when things are going well for you, you might struggle to see the good. This kind of self-doubt is unhealthy. When you cannot see your good qualities, it becomes difficult to stay motivated. You might believe you will never attain your goals, don't have the talent required, or are unworthy of any position you hold. Any small failure you encounter becomes proof of your perceived sense of unworthiness. Unhealthy self-doubt is like a parasite that consumes you from within while reducing your self-worth, self-esteem, and self-efficacy.

There are certain psychological mechanisms used by self-doubt to perpetuate their unhealthy attitudes toward themselves. For instance, if you're worried that you will not pass an exam, you might be tempted not to study at all. By doing this, you can easily associate the blame of your failure to not studying or the lack of preparation. It is quite an innovative way to shift all the blame away from ourselves and onto an external factor. You can reassure yourself by saying that it was not you who failed, but the situation itself that led to your failure. Had you studied harder, you might have passed. Since you didn't study, you did not pass. This kind of belief is self-sabotaging. Since it stems from the fear of failure, you will always be scared. It is also a reason people tend to procrastinate. If you keep at it for too long, you will eventually reach a situation where you believe you cannot succeed because regardless of what you do, failure is the only potential destination.

The way you talk to yourself repeatedly forms certain dents in your neural pathways. If you keep telling yourself you are incapable of doing something or you are not good enough, these thoughts will become a part of your psyche, and you will believe them to be the truth. This self-fulfilling prophecy is based on the notion that "I cannot." When you convince yourself that you cannot do something, the effort you make will also reduce. If you are going to fail, then what is the point in trying? With less effort, you tend to increase your chances of failing, which in turn reinforces your negative beliefs and ends up creating a rather vicious cycle.

If you don't celebrate your achievements, it is because of a lack of self-kindness. You might be supportive and nurturing towards all those you love, yet you may be critical of yourself. The absence or lack of self-kindness leads to self-doubt. When you are kinder to yourself, it becomes easier to embrace your deficiencies and improve yourself. All those individuals who have a higher level of self-doubt often seek approval from others. They tend to worry more about their failures and negatively evaluate all the situations, which leads to unnecessary self-judgment. It also increases the risk of isolation.

Another factor that is associated with self-doubt is impostor syndrome. It describes an unreasonable feeling of being an impostor where, in fact, all the achievements you attained are accredited to luck instead of your personal abilities and effort. You probably believe that it is only a matter of time before others discover that you are a fraud in disguise. Anxiety and depression are commonly accompanied by impostor syndrome. By giving credit to all your achievements to external factors instead of your own self, you prevent yourself from successfully seeing your self-worth.

Overcoming Self-Doubt

William Shakespeare once said that our doubts are traitors, and they make us lose out on all the good in life because we fear failure. Self-doubt not only holds you back from acting on opportunities, but it also makes it difficult to start and finish things. The good news is, you can easily overcome self-doubt, provided you make an effort to create change. Self-doubt stems from the internal negative self-talk and wrong beliefs you have formed about yourself. Here are different steps you can use to overcome self-doubt.

Being Real

It is time to be real with yourself. Ask yourself this simple question, "How many times when I feared the worst did it actually become a reality?" Well, if you are honest, then it might not have happened as often as you thought it would. Self-doubts are like the imaginary monsters that kids fear before going to sleep at night. They tend to prevent you from making any changes and keep you well within your comfort zone. If you want to develop and excel in life, you need to step outside your comfort zone.

Take some time and carefully analyze your past. Think about all the instances where things progressed smoothly despite your doubts. Once you realize that not all your self-doubts are based on facts, it becomes easier to let go.

Stop It

Whenever you feel that your internal self-talk becomes negative, tell yourself to stop. You can control your thoughts. Instead of allowing them to spin out of control, you can quickly discourage them. If you feel yourself questioning your own motives, try to talk to the doubtful part in your psyche. You can easily disrupt any patterns of negative self-talk by telling yourself to stop. You can scream at your internal critic to quit being negative. Don't allow your thoughts to control you. Instead, learn to control your thoughts.

Stop Comparing

If you keep comparing yourself to others or to the successes they have attained, it becomes easier to doubt yourself. Since we live in a world where we are surrounded with constant social media posts about others living the perfect life, it becomes tempting to compare oneself with these projections. Instead of comparing yourself to others, compare yourself to yourself. When you spend some time and analyze your life, you will see all the progress you have made. You are your worst enemy and your best competition. The only person you need to outdo is yourself. Think about all the obstacles you have overcome in your life and all the negative circumstances you have successfully navigated. There might have been some instances in your past where you thought it was the end of the world. Well, it wasn't, and the proof is the fact that you are here today! Congratulate yourself on making it this far and keep pushing forward.

Talk to Someone

When you keep all your thoughts to yourself, they often become distorted and exaggerated. It might also reach a situation where they are no longer reasonable. All this is true with self-doubt. To remove yourself from such a situation, it is always a good idea to talk to someone else about it. Once you let go and say these things out loud, you will hear how exaggerated your self-doubt has become. When you talk to someone you trust and love, you might be able to see things from a different perspective.

People Don't Care

A person with extremely high levels of self-doubt often believes that others think about what they say or do. When you start worrying too much about what others think or say, self-doubt tends to get a stronger hold over you. Whenever this happens, remind yourself that people don't really care that much. After all, everyone has their own lives to deal with. Even if they make any negative remarks, it all stops there.

Things will not bother you unless you permit them to do so. People have to think about themselves, their jobs, or any other aspect of their lives. Since they have all this to do, they won't have that much time to worry about you. So, forget about what others think. It is not your job to change the way others perceive you. As long as you are true to yourself, you have nothing to worry about.

Journalizing

Maintaining a journal is a very good idea in terms of dealing with self-doubt. Maintain a realistic account of your life. Don't forget to include the positive aspects of your life while writing the negative ones. After all, life isn't always that bad. If you look for it, you will realize that there are many things to appreciate in your life. When you start writing down your doubts and fears, it becomes easier to gain a sense of clarity. All the things you are worried about might not seem that catastrophic once you write them down. Apart from this, it also gives you a better perspective of the issue at hand. Whenever you are facing a challenge, start writing the list of pros and cons of different solutions you can use. This is a rational and logical way to deal with a challenge instead of worrying about failure.

Not Always About You

Regardless of what you might choose to believe, everything isn't always about you. Whenever someone criticizes you, it is easy to start doubting yourself. When someone rejects you on a date, it is difficult not to take it personally. However, what if the things others said were never about you? Perhaps your boss criticized you because he was having a bad day at home. The guy you were on a date with didn't want to go on another date because he was still hung up on his ex.

Perhaps he had other commitments to deal with. When you think about all the incidents in your life from the perspective of someone else, you will realize that the world doesn't revolve around you. Instead of readily accepting blame for everything, analyze the situation from the other person's perspective.

Setbacks are Temporary

Nothing in life is permanent. Even if it feels like you're going through an incredibly tough time right now, it will pass. A setback is a temporary situation, and you have the power to overcome it. Keep in mind that you are not a failure because you failed in a specific situation. The true failure is when you refuse to learn from your experiences. Everything that happens in your life happens for a reason. Once you understand the reason, you will be a better version of yourself.

Start following these simple, practical tips, and you will see a change in your internal attitude toward yourself and life.

Chapter Five: 21 Things Confident Women DON'T Do

When you think of some confident women like Oprah Winfrey, Malala Yousafzai, Meghan Markle, or even Hillary Clinton, what do these ladies have in common that makes them so fearless in life? They all carry themselves with an air of unapologetic grace, success, and unfettered determination. The energy changes whenever they enter the room. In this section, let us look at a couple of mistakes you must avoid if you wish to become a confident woman and how you measure up in terms of self-confidence.

1. Don't Give in to Self-Doubt

Self-doubt is common, but a confident woman knows not to pay attention to unnecessary self-doubt. Hesitation is not a natural part of how they process things, and they seldom second-guess their own decisions. They often know what they are doing and the reasons for doing them. They spend the time required to think about their decisions thoroughly, and once they have decided, nothing can stop them.

2. Don't Worry About Trends

A confident woman is not someone who follows trends but is a trendsetter. Don't waste your time thinking about what is "in" or what society thinks you should to do. Instead, all the choices you make must be based on your personal preferences. Confident women are well aware of their needs and preferences. They don't hesitate to ask for what they want, because they believe they deserve everything that they want.

3. Don't Waste Time Gossiping

Nothing wastes time quite like gossip. Confident women don't talk about other women and don't waste their time gossiping. Instead, they focus all their time and energy on talking about their goals, dreams, plans, and aspirations.

4. Not All Opinions Matter

Everyone has an opinion, but a confident woman understands not to base her decisions on what others think or feel. She might listen to others, but every decision she makes is based on her own conclusions. She will never listen to any advice blindly, rather, she will do her own fact-finding to understand what she must or must not do.

5. Don't Suppress Your Feelings

Confident women don't attempt to suppress their feelings. If there's something on their minds, rest easy knowing that you will know it. They are not worried about calling things as they see it. With confidence comes the ability to speak one's mind freely and openly in a way that others will listen to.

6. Don't Worry About Pleasing Others

Confident women are not people pleasers. If they want to do something, they will do it. They are self-assured, and their self-confidence is not based on external sources of approval. They are true to themselves and fully trust their intuition. A confident woman not only has the ability to hear her heart but also has the strength to handle any opposition. Since she doesn't waste all her time trying to make others happy, she is a happier person.

7. Don't Ignore Self-Care

A confident woman knows that she is responsible for her wellbeing. She would never compromise on self-care. She understands the importance of maintaining a balance between her personal and professional life. She takes the time required to eat healthy meals, sleep properly, and even spend time pampering herself. She does all this because she knows it is in her best interest.

8. Don't Have Any Regrets

Confident women not only learn their lessons from their past experiences, but also understand all the mistakes and poor choices they might have made. They do this having no regrets. The ability to learn from the past and improve oneself is a sign of self-confidence. Instead of wasting their time worrying about all the things they could have done differently, they know what they are supposed to do.

9. Don't Confuse Failure with Defeat

Confident women don't think of failure as the ultimate defeat. They know that every failure they come across is merely a stepping-stone to success. They are the ones who will tell you the number of times Henry Ford went bankrupt before he became extremely successful. They understand that the path to success is never smooth, and there are plenty of bumps along the way. They experience failure like everyone else, but they also know how to learn from their mistakes and keep moving forward.

10. It is Okay to Get Messy

A confident woman knows that it is okay to get messy. Even if they value making good first impressions and like to look good, they don't care if they get their hands dirty to attain their goals. They will not be bothered if they are caught in a rainstorm or get dirt on their hands while tending to their needs. They know how to look at the positive in every situation regardless of whether they are stuck in a horrible downpour or experience a nasty fall.

11. Don't Forget your Purpose

Confident women understand their purpose in life and use this to guide all the decisions they make. They are not the ones who would go about their day like a headless chicken. Instead, these determined women know precisely what they want and how they can attain their goals. Once they have a goal in mind, nothing can stop them. They don't make any unconscious decisions, and every risk taken is calculated. This fearless way in which they live their lives is what makes them extremely magnetic to others.

12. Don't Worry about Peer Pressure

Giving in to peer pressure is something many people do, especially the ones who don't have their own opinions or beliefs. These people always give in to what others want them to do. Since confident women understand what they want without trying to please others, it is easier for them to avoid the stress of peer pressure. Peer pressure is reserved for people who worry too much about what others think. A confident woman doesn't have the time to indulge in this unnecessary worry.

13. Always Be Productive

Productivity is often confused with being busy. You can be busy doing a hundred different things, but it doesn't mean you are productive. Productivity is making the most of the time and resources available to you in order to attain any objectives you set for yourself. A confident woman knows not to glorify this aspect of being busy. Confident women are productive and always concentrate on getting the job done. Since they are getting things done, they don't feel overwhelmed by all the tasks they have to accomplish.

14. Don't Ignore Your Instincts

Even if everyone thinks one thing, or facts point to something different, confident women will always go with their intuition. They know that they are not supposed to ignore what their instincts are telling them. Intuition is the little voice in your head that tells you that something may be amiss. If something doesn't feel right and your gut says so, then pay heed to it. When it comes to decision-making, gut instinct is your biggest ally. Confident women not only understand this but aren't scared to trust their gut. Your intuition or gut instinct is based on a millennium of evolution and tries to protect you in any dangerous situation. Ignoring your gut instinct is not something you should do.

15. Silence isn't Uncomfortable

Silence doesn't have to be uncomfortable, and a confident woman knows this. She knows how to be content even when there is no one around. Her source of comfort is internalized and not based on any external sources. She has the awareness to accept herself and her thoughts. Therefore, silence seldom bothers her. Silence only bothers those who cannot deal with their thoughts. If you make peace with your thoughts, you will feel comfortable too.

16. Don't Take Everything Personally

Confident women know not to take others' opinions personally. They know that everyone is entitled to their opinions and that the opinion of others doesn't reflect poorly on them. They might value the input from others but will not be too bothered if such opinions don't support their personal beliefs. If you take everything that everyone says personally, then you will merely make yourself unhappy. In the end, the only person who will feel bad is you.

17. Don't Fret Over Materialistic Possessions

A confident woman knows better than to equate who she is as a person with what she has. Confident women don't allow materialistic possessions to define who they are. They may or may not live in the swankiest houses or use the latest gadgets because they know their self-worth. Instead of allowing petty possessions to define them, they define themselves. They live their lives based on what they want and not live how others think they should.

18. Quality and not Quantity

Confident women know the value of authenticity. In fact, they will value it more than being popular. Instead of having hundreds of friends and millions of followers on social media, they value authentic relationships they share with a select few. Quality always comes before quantity for confident women. They love challenging conversations and don't aspire to be popular because they know it doesn't matter in the end.

19. Don't Need External Motivation

Confident women don't need others to support or believe in them. They have the internal motivation and the desire to succeed. They know what needs to be done. They are their personal cheerleaders. They don't need personal trainers or alarm clocks to motivate them to do things they need to do. Their internal motivation drives them to get a jump on the day without hitting any snooze buttons. The kind of clarity they have about their desires and wants gives them the motivation and the courage to work toward achieving them.

20. Don't Deny Yourself

A confident woman knows not to deny herself. She understands that there needs to be balance in every aspect of life. Apart from this, she also knows that every function has a limit. She will never try to stretch herself thin or push herself to her breaking point unnecessarily. She will try to improve herself continuously but will not take on any unnecessary stress. She knows that to be truly happy, she must not deny herself. So, even if she is on a diet, she will not feel guilty for occasionally treating herself to ice cream. She might love going to the gym regularly, but she knows the world will not end if she doesn't exercise for a day. She knows what she wants and will unapologetically work towards attaining those goals.

21. Don't Chase Perfection

Not everything in your life will go exactly in the manner that you have planned. There will be setbacks. Things happen. We might mess things up. Obsessing too much over things and making your happiness dependent on outcomes will do you no good whatsoever. You will need to learn to be happy despite your circumstance. We tend to get in our own way. We do this without realizing it. You will need to quit worrying about a specific outcome. Things will happen, and there will be things that are beyond your control. The only thing you can control is your actions. You cannot control the situations you are in. You should stop worrying about getting a specific result. Instead, concentrate on how you can make most of what's given to you. If you try too hard to get a certain result, you will get in your own way. Desperation will not get you the results you want. It will just hinder your growth. Stop trying to fit in where you don't belong. If the shoe doesn't fit, it is time to move on. Find something that you are comfortable in.

Confident women know that others don't have to like them. Perhaps this is one of the main reasons why everyone seems to like them and aspire to be them. Now that you've gone through the list of things that confident women **don't do**, it will become easier to gauge yourself. If you notice that you do certain things that these women don't do, then take action today to change yourself.

Chapter Six: 7 Confidence Hacks

Did you ever notice that some people seem more confident than others? It might also feel like confidence is an inherent trait that only a select few have been blessed with. Well, this isn't true. Confidence is a skill much like any other. So, even if you lack self-confidence, you can easily work on improving yourself. It takes time, commitment, patience, and plenty of conscious effort to develop this trait. However, once you get the hang of it, your confidence levels will soar! In this chapter, let us look at practical tips you can follow to improve your levels of confidence.

Hack #1: Act 'As If'

Did you ever come across the phrase "Smell your fear"? Well, fictional characters and people in the real-life often talk about animals and humans smell fear on others. It can conjure up images of a snarling dog or a knife-wielding psychopath. Yes, humans can smell fear. Human communication doesn't take place just via spoken word, but also visual means. Friends, loved ones, customers, potential business partners, and other prospects can smell your fear.

You probably think you're putting on a good facade to come across as being confident while engaging in conversation with others, or even while making a presentation. However, if you don't feel genuinely confident about yourself, then people can see through your facade, and they can see your lack of confidence. It can be extremely harmful to your ability to succeed because people will not believe you if you don't believe in yourself. Confidence is a very contagious emotion. If you don't feel confident about yourself, you cannot expect others to feel confident about you. For instance, no one will want to engage in a business prospect with you if you don't feel confident about yourself and the business that you are trying to start.

We all face circumstances where we doubt ourselves. Even the most confident people experience self-doubt from time to time. It is natural to doubt yourself, especially when you find yourself in an unfamiliar situation or around strangers.

Confidence is like a big balloon that can either soar high in the sky or deflate depending on how you feel about yourself. Your confidence can take a backseat, especially if the criticism comes from someone you love or respect. For instance, a child in school can feel absolutely crushed if her favorite music teacher tells her that she cannot play the lead in a musical because of her weight or her body type. Even if the child was never conscious of such a thing until the incident, she would certainly become conscious of herself later.

Keep in mind that your parents cannot revive your confidence for you, and even your friends cannot. They can certainly make you feel better, but confidence needs to come from within. You cannot expect others to make you feel confident. Likewise, if your confidence stems from external sources, then it can get shattered easily. Confidence is a state of mind. Much like happiness, the key to feeling more confident is in your hands. If you are willing to work on yourself, you can become as confident as you want.

If you have a goal, don't quit, as you need to keep going. Whenever you take on something new, doubt and fear start cropping up in your mind. It is a signal that you're supposed to take stock of your inventory of skills and knowledge to ensure that you can succeed. Whenever these feelings signal that you are missing something important, pay attention to them. Missing an important piece of information or skills can lead to a potential disaster. For instance, you can electrocute yourself trying to rewire the house if you don't know what you're supposed to be doing.

At times, these feelings and signals can be misleading. Fear and doubt crop up while you are learning something new or are trying to grow in life. These kinds of experiences are quintessential for success, like when you take on a project you have never attempted before or are trying to learn something new for the first time.

So, how can you develop confidence in situations like these? How can you show that you are confident when you don't feel confident? The only way to feel more confident is by overcoming your fear and self-doubt. Two important factors create self-confidence. The first factor is to believe in the project, as it should be in line with your dreams. The second factor is to believe that you have what it takes to attain your objectives. The first factor is relatively easy to deal with when compared to the second one. If someone somewhere else at some point has done something you are trying to attain, then your goal is achievable. Now, this brings us to the second part of the equation, which is relatively tricky, because when you have the required skill, knowledge, and abilities, you might not have enough confidence in yourself. If you want to be successful in life, then you need to understand there is always a certain risk involved in everything that you do. You cannot grow or attain your goals in life if you don't take on risks. Even if you believe you can succeed, there will be risks involved. So, make your peace with this and take the first step. However, don't take any foolish risks, always take calculated risks.

The simplest way to begin feeling more confident is to use the 'act as if' technique. This technique mainly uses your natural mental and emotional responses to bring about thoughts and behavior that will make you feel more confident. When you don't feel confident about something or yourself, your mind concludes that despite the circumstances, you are a beyond your abilities or understanding. The physical response of your body to these thoughts is to become tense, and your mind responds to it by digging up memories along with thoughts that reaffirm the fears and doubts you have.

Your emotions might further the perception that the circumstances you are in are bigger than you can handle, and it restarts the cycle once again. It is a cycle of natural response that connects your basic thoughts and actions. The 'act as if' technique helps reverse this reaction cycle by changing the way you think and the way you act. If you want to increase your confidence, then you need to behave like you are confident. So, let us start with your posture. When you are running low on confidence, your body mirrors your state of mind, and you tend to shrink or slouch unknowingly. Instead, make a conscious effort to sit with your back straight and keep your shoulders held high. Lift your chin and always look straight ahead instead of slouching.

Next, concentrate on your breathing. Taking in shallow and rapid breaths is a sign of hyperventilation and nervousness. Once you start breathing calmly and deeply through your nose and slowly exhale, your body will start to relax. After changing your posture and the way you breathe, you will be more relaxed. Continue this process by opting for clothes that reflect what you are trying to attain. Start behaving, thinking, and talking as if you have already attained the goal you want.

For inspiration, you can always look at those who have achieved the goals you want. Pay attention to the way they behave, walk, and talk. If you're not able to understand what you're supposed to do, then you can copy them. Imitate the way they talk and walk. It doesn't mean that you have to mimic every single aspect of the personality, just copy those things that spell confidence. The final step to this exercise is to think about yourself differently. It is time to shush your inner critic and change the way you talk to yourself. Instead of wasting your time thinking about all those memories that reinforce your self-doubt and fear, think about all the circumstances in your past when you overcame challenges and attained your goals.

Here's a simple affirmation you can use whenever you feel a little low on confidence. "This is a new challenge I am facing, but I have overcome difficult obstacles in the past." Reinforce your self-confidence by telling yourself that you have all the skills and knowledge you require to get the job done. Even if you don't have the skills right now, tell yourself you can always learn about them as you progress.

Once you start behaving as if you have attained your goals, your emotions will start to settle, you will be able to relax, and you can think about all the challenges that lie ahead of you. When your mind starts believing that every circumstance you are in is perfectly manageable, it becomes easier to feel more confident. Concentrate on consciously encouraging your mind to reinforce positive thoughts and emotions. Armed with the feelings of confidence and boldness, you will soon be able to take the necessary steps required to attain your goal, and within no time, you no longer have to 'act.'

This technique doesn't work if you are trying to pretend to be confident. People can see right through any facade that you put up. This technique works because it instils confidence in yourself by changing your perception or perspective of the situation you are in. If you think something is unattainable, then attaining it will become difficult because you believe it to be impossible. It essentially helps reprogram your mind and the nervous system to respond favorably toward any challenges without creating any dents in your self-confidence. This technique is not the only way in which you can become more confident. However, it is one of the simplest ways in which you can become more confident, and it is easy to follow.

So, whenever you are running low on confidence, remind yourself that you are a confident woman who can achieve whatever she puts her mind to. Consciously correct your posture, breathing, and your actions. By following these three simple steps, you will start to feel more confident and in control of your life.

The 'act as if' technique can not only be used to improve your level of self-confidence, but it works very well for other emotions as well. If you want to be happy, then start acting happy. Think happy thoughts and behave in ways that happy people usually do. Always keep a smile on your face, hold your head high, enjoy yourself, play, and have some fun. If you do all these things, eventually, you will feel happier. This technique is based on the law of attraction. The law merely states that you receive what you give out to the universe. So, if you send positive vibes out into the universe, the universe sends positive vibes back to you.

Hack #2: Spruce Yourself Up

You've probably heard the saying that beauty is just skin deep. Well, inner beauty matters more than outer beauty, but looks do matter. When you look good, you tend to feel better about yourself. Various factors directly influence your self-esteem, and physical appearance is one of them. Any perceived flaws you have about your looks could be a source of distress. In extreme cases, it can lead to mental disorders like social anxiety, eating disorders, or even body Dysmorphic disorder. In simple terms, low self-confidence about your looks can adversely affect your overall mood. So, let us look at simple ways in which you can spruce yourself up to improve your level of self-confidence.

Improving your appearance

The first step is to figure out the triggers that affect your confidence. Do you feel more confident when you dress a certain way? Do you feel less confident when you don't spend enough time to groom yourself? Is your confidence dependent upon the group you spend more time with? Are there any other issues like your relationship status, or your employment status that trigger low self-confidence? Your self-perception sometimes triggers low self-confidence.

The second step is to concentrate on the way you perceive your physical appearance. Think about your source of self-esteem, question any negative beliefs you have about your looks, and think of ways in which you can change your beliefs about your physical appearance. While analyzing all these things, start writing down your observations.

Make a note of three things that you like most about your physical appearance, and three things about your personality that you like the most. It could be something as simple as volunteering at a local charity or maybe even calling your friends right away when they need someone to talk to. If you don't appreciate yourself, you cannot expect others to appreciate you. You need to love and respect yourself unconditionally if you want to change the way you think about yourself.

Humans are vain, but not a lot of people accept this. It is perhaps one reason why most of us talk about having a wonderful personality more than looks. It is okay to concentrate on personality traits, but it is not okay to forget about physical appearance.

Now, it is time to make a list of your three best personality features. Maybe you love your curly hair, your limbs, or even your smile. Make a list of your three physical features that you love the most. It is time for a little self-introspection. Stand in front of a full-length mirror and think about all the different thoughts that come into your mind the minute you see your reflection. Are all these thoughts based on your self-perception, or are they based on the opinion of others? Try to understand the accuracy of the opinions that have been made about you. Are you taller than others? Are your hips wider than others? Are you too skinny? Do any of these things matter?

If one of your friends came to you because she was having a body image crisis, how would you talk to her? Would you try to reassure her or criticize her? If you are compassionate toward others, then it is time to extend the same compassion toward yourself. Concentrate on replacing all negative thoughts with positive ones. Instead of concentrating on your perceived negative attributes, concentrate on the positive ones.

We are constantly bombarded by different images or notions of the perfect and ideal body on social media. Keep in mind that just because someone perceives something to be the perfect body type, it doesn't mean you need to live up to the same perception. Most of the images of celebrities you see these days have been thoroughly airbrushed and photoshopped. Don't try to live up to an unrealistic perception of beauty. Work on reframing positive thoughts about your body. For instance, if you think that your nose is too big or your eyes are too small, remind yourself that these features make you unique.

Make a habit of writing at least three positive things you love about yourself. Before going to sleep every night, record these thoughts in a journal, and keep doing this daily. It will be a positive journal. So, whenever you start feeling low on self-confidence, you can quickly go through your journal and feel better about yourself.

Changing your style

Researchers at the Harvard Medical School in the USA conducted a study, along with the University at Chieti in Italy, to test the influence make-up can have on women. One hundred and eighty-six women took part in this study, and it was conducted to determine whether the "lipstick effect" is a true phenomenon or not. The lipstick effect is used to describe a psychological phenomenon where a woman feels more confident and attractive when she wears make-up. Well, the study showed that women feel more confident after wearing make-up that suits them. So, it is safe to say that your level of self-confidence also depends upon how you feel about yourself. By merely changing your style, you can feel more confident.

Start wearing clothes that make you feel comfortable. You don't have to compromise on style for the sake of comfort or compromise on comfort for the sake of style. Start by recognizing your unique sense of style and dress accordingly. Certain trends and styles might look good on celebrities and models but might not necessarily suit you. So, learn to recognize what does and doesn't suit you and dress accordingly. You don't have to follow the latest trends to look good blindly.

The clothes you wear must highlight the physical features you favor. Always dress according to your body shape and learn how to flatter your body shape. There are different basic body shapes and understanding the various types of clothes that accentuate your best features means you can dress in a way that suits you. For instance, avoid wearing dark colors and monochrome if you are skinny. If you have broad shoulders and long limbs, then wear clothes that concentrate on your limbs! It is simple, but it takes a little preparation.

Start wearing well-tailored clothes or the ones that fit you well. Even a gorgeous woman can look like a sack of potatoes if she wears ill-fitting clothes. If you find no clothes that fit you well, then you can always get them tailored.

Wearing the right shade of lipstick and applying the right kinds of make-up can make you feel better about yourself. Choose the right color of lipstick based on your lip color. For instance, bright shades of red and pink-colored lipsticks look good on women who have pale lips, and warmer shades look good on the ones who have dark lips. While applying make-up, ensure that you are using make-up based on your face shape. For instance, if you have a rather rounded face, then use make-up to define your cheeks and eyes instead of concentrating on your lips. There are different tricks you can use to uplift your natural features instantly. In fact, there are plenty of YouTube tutorials and videos you can use for inspiration.

Get a good haircut that matches your face shape and highlights your natural beauty. Just because bangs look chic on your favorite actress doesn't mean they will suit you. If you have a square face or a strong jawline, then getting layers to frame your face will help soften the sharp facial lines you have.

Spend some time and concentrate on keeping yourself well-groomed. Create a daily, weekly, and monthly grooming routine for yourself. Ensure that you always keep your nails clean and well-trimmed. You don't necessarily have to get a manicure every ten days, but it is entirely up to you. Brush your teeth at least twice a day to improve your oral health and hygiene. Always carry wet wipes with you to freshen up, even while traveling. Drink plenty of water to keep your skin thoroughly hydrated. Apart from this, invest in the right beauty products like concealer, bronzer, an eye shadow palette, lipstick, and so on based on your skin tone. Start washing, moisturizing, and cleansing your face before going to bed at night. Using a good fragrance can also instantly change the way you feel about yourself.

Experiment with different styles until you find one that works well for you. It is a process of trial and error, so be a little patient.

Regardless of who you are, or the state of life you are in, you always have the power to make yourself feel better. Don't give up on yourself and don't fall into a cycle of self-loathing. If you want to feel your best, then you need to look your best. When you feel positive about yourself, then the way you look at life will also change. There is nothing frivolous about beauty. It is quite empowering and can positively influence your state of mind. Feeling good about yourself is powerful. There is a direct relationship that exists between your inner and the outer beauty-the way you think about yourself is the way others think about you. Beauty can be used to bring about a positive change in your life and start using it today.

Your self-confidence is greatly influenced by the way you perceive yourself and your physical appearance. By following these simple steps, you can improve your physical appearance. Not just your physical appearance, it also creates a positive change in the way you perceive yourself. Once you are happy and satisfied with the way you look, you will feel more confident. Apart from this, simple tips will also ensure that you are taking good care of yourself. Self-care is also important for self-confidence.

Hack #3: Think Like a Goddess

You might have come across different quotes on the Internet, or social media like "You are a goddess, just remind yourself of it." These quotes are supposed to be motivating and inspirational. However, the message that they send seems to be along the lines of, "You are flawless, and you don't have to work on yourself." Well, this isn't true. We all have flaws and accepting them is important. There is always a scope for improvement. Believing oneself to be flawless differs from loving oneself despite the flaws.

Hearing that you are amazing or awesome doesn't cause any changes within us, even when we know it isn't the truth. As soon as you hear the truth, you might not want to hear it. Being criticized by others or our inner critics is seldom pleasant. Well, nobody is perfect, and you don't have to be perfect. Don't try to be.

By allocating a self-care day, taking a bubble bath, or spending hours together at the spa might make you feel better. However, all this is just fleeting, and self-care is so much more than this. Self-care is about an attitude and mindset instead of a bubble bath and pedicures. Taking care of your physical, mental, and emotional wellbeing must be your priority. Look at your reflection in the mirror and tell yourself certain positive attributes about your body. Self-care is not a destination, and it is an ongoing journey. If you want to feel confident about yourself, or anything you have achieved, then it takes time, effort, and patience. To feel confident, you will need to work on yourself. By meditating for an hour or spending the day at the spa, you cannot feel confident. It must be an ongoing thing.

Everyone keeps talking about accepting one as a goddess. What does the Goddess mindset even mean? The truth is, it isn't the lack of capability, skills, experience that tends to hold most of us back from attaining our goals. It is about having the right emotional mindset. This mindset is known as the Goddess mindset. It is based on the simple belief that you need to believe you are worth it. It needs to be one of your core beliefs. A Goddess mindset is about creating a positive belief in yourself and tapping into your internal goddess. It is about learning to harness the energy that is present within yourself to improve your confidence. It is about loving yourself unconditionally and cherishing your body, mind, and soul.

Unless you truly embody the goddess that you are, you cannot unlock your actual potential. There is so much more to you than the mere tags the society uses to describe you. You could be someone's daughter, mother, wife, sister, granddaughter, friend, confidant, and so on. Well, you are more than these tags describe. You need to understand that you are all this and much more. The way you feel about yourself determines the kind of energy and people you attract into your life. Once you learn to awaken and embrace your inner goddess, you will feel unstoppable.

There are many different things that can destroy your self-confidence. It could be because of any family issues, turbulence in your professional life, or the simple perception that you are not enough. Someone could probably look at you in a way that makes you uncomfortable. Various people in the form of bullies, unfaithful lovers, abusive co-workers, or troublesome bosses can bring you down. Situations can also bring you down, such as not getting the job you wanted, dealing with a divorce or a breakup, or being ghosted by a person that you thought you connected with. Pretty much anything under the sun can affect your level of confidence. When all these things develop over the years, confidence tends to take a backseat. It distracts you from connecting with your natural goddess.

Regardless of whether you find your soulmate, the perfect house, the perfect job, or even live the perfect life, learning to accept your inner goddess is important. Reconnecting with your inner goddess and finally understanding the goddess mindset will help you regain your confidence. Allow no one to tell you that you don't deserve to live the kind of life you want. If you truly want something, then the entire universe will help make it come true.

Here are the simple steps you can use to reconnect with your inner goddess.

Start believing in yourself. See yourself for who you truly are and work on improving yourself every day. Try to be the best version of yourself and always put your best foot forward. It doesn't mean you need to hide your insecurities or your flaws. In fact, it means the exact opposite of it. It means you need to embrace yourself, and every aspect of your being. If you don't like something about yourself, you can always work on changing it. A goddess is someone who doesn't doubt herself, her capabilities, or her beauty.

Don't hide your flaws or ignore them. Learn to accept your flaws and love them because they make you who you are. Your flaws make you unique. Don't try to chase the mirage of perfection. Instead, be the kind of person you want to be. Do these things for yourself and not because of what others say or think.

Start wearing clothes that make you feel confident and sexy. Don't worry about what society will think or say. People will talk regardless of what you do. Instead of holding yourself back, unleash your inner goddess.

The environment you surround yourself with reflects your beliefs. You probably have certain dreams based on the good feeling you think will be yours one day when you attain your dreams, right? The trick to manifest that good feeling associated with the dream into reality is by feeling good at this moment. You don't have to wait for an uncertain future to feel good; you can start feeling good this instant. This good feeling will help you attract good into your life.

Do your surroundings at work and home reflect your sense of style and make you feel good right now? If they don't, then it is time to work on improving your environment immediately. You can start by decluttering so that your space is dedicated to only those things that add value to your life and help achieve your dreams. It is about allowing the free flow of energy around you. When you are surrounded by an environment conducive to good vibes, you will automatically feel good.

Add all those things that inspire and motivate you and eliminate everything else. Don't clutter yourself with unnecessary things. Decluttering is a great way to prioritize your needs and wants. When your surroundings are well organized, it brings about a sense of order and clarity. These positive aspects will have a positive effect on the way you think. For instance, a cluttered desk might stifle your creativity. So, unclutter to unleash your inner goddess.

You need to talk like a goddess as well. It is not just the way you talk to others; your self-talk matters. Most of us are good at criticizing, comparing, and judging ourselves. All this kind of negative dialogue tends to cause more harm than good. It is okay to take some time for self-introspection and understand the different aspects of your life you would like to change. However, indulging in excessive self-criticism will harm your self-esteem and self-confidence. Negative self-talk leads to unnecessary damage of any issue you are dealing with. This kind of criticism can also prevent you from thinking rationally and clearly. If you're in a critic keeps telling you that you are not good enough or that you are not enough, you will soon start believing that as well. Get rid of all disempowering thoughts and beliefs. To do this, you need to pay attention to what you think and your internal self-talk. Once you start regulating it and replace all negative beliefs with positive ones, it is empowering.

Whenever you notice any self-sabotaging thoughts pop into your head, try to change it. Initially, it takes plenty of conscious effort, but after a while, it will come to you naturally. For instance, what is your first reaction whenever you are faced with an obstacle? Do you believe that the obstacles are the end of the road or that you will not be able to overcome them? Well, this is just negative thinking at play. Instead, think of it as an opportunity to learn and grow. Maybe there is a chance that has been presented to you in life to improve yourself. Keep in mind that everything that happens in life happens for a reason. If you look hard enough, then you will realize that every cloud has a silver lining. It is merely about the way you view and perceive things.

Another great way to bring about positivity into your life is via positive affirmations. Start using daily affirmations to reaffirm your self-confidence. The simple daily affirmations you can use are as follows:

- I am a confident woman.
- I am brilliant.
- I accept and embrace my flaws because they make me who I am.
- I am an incredibly sexy woman.
- I love the person I am.
- I am grateful for every experience I have had, both good and bad, because they define me.

Money is certainly an important aspect of life. Ignoring it or believing that it is unnecessary is rather naïve. However, it is important to understand that money is not everything. That being said, it is an important factor that contributes to the way you feel about yourself and the confidence you have in yourself. How do you feel about prosperity and your finances? Are you one knowingly sabotaging the flow of money into your life because you don't see it in your bank balance right now? This tends to happen whenever you unintentionally dishonor whatever you have right now by believing that what you have is not sufficient.

If you believe that you have no money, or that you will never have enough finances, then you are not attracting positivity into your life. Therefore, it is time to replace all this with a little positivity. Dealing with your finances is an overwhelming task, and it is difficult. The simplest way to go about doing this is by keeping track of every single penny that comes your way. Even if a penny doesn't seem like much right now, but they all add up, and eventually it fattens up your bank balance.

Learn to understand your worth and work on improving yourself. Always keep a positive attitude in life and don't let any negativity bring you down. Every negative encounter or experience you have in life is a learning lesson. Don't allow it to extinguish the power of your inner goddess. Embrace the goddess mindset, and you will see a positive change in your overall life and attitude toward life.

Hack #4: Crack a Smile

You might have heard the lyrics of an old song that goes something like, "When you are smiling, the whole world smiles with you." Well, it turns out this song is right, and smiles are quite contagious. Yes, you read it right - smiles are contagious. When you see someone smile at you, don't you smile at them automatically? It is a knee-jerk reaction that takes even if you don't know the other person.

We all have different subconscious needs, and perhaps the deepest emotional need of all is the need for self-esteem. A vital means via which the subconscious need for self-esteem can be fulfilled is through acceptance. Who would not want to be liked and accepted just the way they are without changing anything? One of the major reasons for lack of self-esteem and self-confidence these days is the lack of acceptance or rejection from certain groups are individuals and society. If you keep expressing your unconditional acceptance of every person you meet - not just at home, but even at work - you will soon be amongst the most popular people across the world. How can you express your unconditional acceptance? Well, start smiling.

It only takes 12 facial muscles to smile, whereas it takes 113 facial muscles to frown. Whenever you genuinely smile at someone, it conveys a positive message that the said person is pleasant, likable, or even attractive. A single smile is so powerful that it can quickly uplift someone else's low self-esteem. Not just that, when you smile, you are sending positive vibes across to someone. It kicks starts the reaction when that person sends positive vibes your way. And the cycle keeps going on.

Make a conscious habit of smiling as much and as often as you can. While smiling, ensure that your smiles are genuine and not faked or forced. People can see through a fake smile. It doesn't take much to smile, and it is quite a simple thing to do. If you are unable to smile, then think about a couple of positive thoughts and experiences you had in your life, or even the people who make you laugh, and a smile will automatically appear on your lips.

Whenever you smile at anyone else, it kickstarts a physical reaction where endorphins are released in your body. Endorphins are feel-good hormones that instantly elevate your mood. These endorphins not only make you feel happy, but they also improve your self-esteem. When you smile, you start thinking and even start acting in a way that is more personable to all those around you and give out positive energy. A common behavior that a lot of popular and influential people share is that they always have a genuine smile pasted on their face. Whenever you smile, you are not only making others feel good, but you are also actively improving your self-esteem. This is also an important factor that determines your ability to have healthy and lasting relationships in your life. You cannot have a healthy relationship with someone if you don't smile. It all starts with a smile, and there is no end to the different benefits you stand to gain.

All it takes is one deliberate decision to smile at the people around you and to express that you are genuinely happy to have met or seen them. Being negative will certainly not make you popular. In fact, people will not be comfortable approaching you if you don't smile or have a glum look on your face all the time. The thing with human beings is that we all tend to take everything personally. Even if you look cranky or grumpy for no reason, others might think that someone has done something to upset you. So, to avoid all these unnecessary misunderstandings, it is better just to smile.

Whenever you find yourself a little low on energy or need a little extra motivation, try smiling. Take a couple of minutes out of your routine and think about all the things in your life you are truly grateful for. It could include worldly possessions and all the people you cherish and value. Once you start counting your blessings and express your gratitude, a smile is bound to show up on your lips.

Several researchers have long compiled the list of benefits associated with smiling. It is believed that smiling can make you look a lot younger than you are. Even if there is no other benefit from smiling, this might prompt a lot of people to try to smile more often. Whenever you smile, others tend to perceive you as being a little younger than you are. When you smile, it adds a sparkle to your eye, and this is probably the reason why you look a lot younger. Also, smiling is like giving your face a mini facelift. It turns up the corners of your mouth and raises your entire face including your neck, jowls, and your cheeks. Instead of wasting precious money on getting cosmetic procedures and facelift, it is better to opt for a natural solution that is smiling. If you don't want to look like you are burdened by the troubles of the entire world, then smile and do it often.

When the corners of the mouth are turned down into a frown, it probably gives the impression that you are weighed down by plenty of unhappiness. Why give off a negative impression to someone else? Everyone has their own problems, and everyone is dealing with them. The easiest solution to this problem is to smile.

It is believed that smiling can improve your overall sense of wellbeing while elevating your mood. As mentioned earlier, smiling releases endorphins in your brain. Apart from this, serotonin and dopamine also releases into your system. These hormones directly influence your mood and uplift the way you feel. Endorphins share similar properties with opiates, and they are your body's natural defense against pain. So, the phrase, "smile through your pain," is quite true. You can reduce your body's perception of pain when your nervous system is overrun with feel-good hormones.

The kind of pleasure that smiling induces in your brain is quite similar to the one you feel whenever you eat chocolate. So, you can be quite happy without consuming any extra calories and improve your mood. You no longer have to depend on food to make you happy. All that you need to do is smile a little more. Smiling is simple, and it helps you feel better about yourself.

Even if it is not a natural smile, even for a smile can act as a mood boost. Whenever you think about the positive experiences you have had in life or any happy memories, you tend to smile. By merely deciding to smile, you tend to give your mind a positive experience to concentrate on. The source of your joy doesn't have to be anything else other than your smile. So, if you feel a little blue, smile and instantly uplift your mood. You might have heard others tell you to put on a happy face. Turns out, putting on a happy face actually makes you feel happier.

Apart from all this, smiling tends to make you seem more likable, courteous, and competent. If you seem scared, worried, sad, or anxious, then others might wonder what is troubling you. If you want to seem more confident, then start smiling. It is a simple psychological trick that makes others trust you. For instance, if you have a major presentation that you are worried about, don't frown. By smiling, you are immediately sending a message across to the audience that you know what you are doing and that you are confident about yourself. Fake it 'til you make it, right?

Smiling will not only make you feel better about yourself, but it can make others feel better about themselves, too. If you notice that one of your coworkers is having a hard day at work, why don't you smile at him? You don't have to do anything else, just try sending a few positive vibes to him.

Now that you understand the direct relationship between smiling and your self-confidence, it is time to smile more often. However, there are some things you must consciously try to avoid. You can fake a smile or two, but don't mask all your emotions by smiling. Always analyze your emotions before you decide what to do about them. It is never okay to ignore or forget about any emotions you feel. If you don't deal with your emotions constructively, they all tend to bubble up to the surface and come out negatively. To avoid any unnecessary emotional outburst, try to understand what you are feeling and the reasons for the same. Once you have carefully analyzed all this, then you can decide whether or not you want to smile.

If someone smiles at you, can you discern between a fake and a genuine smile? If you can do this, then others can do it too. There is a distinct difference between a genuine and a fake smile. If your smiles are genuine, you will feel better about yourself, but it will also make you seem more genuine and personable to another person. If you don't want to come across as being fake, then try to control the fake smiles you display.

A smirk differs greatly from a smile. Be aware of how your face looks when you smile. If you keep smirking, you'll come across as being unapproachable. This is not what you're trying to do, is it? If you have heard someone say wipe that smile off your face, then maybe you should look at the way your face looks when you smile. Work on projecting a smile that says you are happy - and also confident.

In certain situations, smiling can seem a little submissive. Just because you are smiling, doesn't mean you need to agree with what others have to say. Even if something displeases you, you can convey your displeasure while smiling. You don't have to try and please everyone else, but there is a way in which you can let others down gently.

Hack #5: Use Power Poses

The idea of power poses has been steadily gaining popularity in recent years. Unless you have been completely off-grid, you will have heard this phrase. Power poses are body postures that are designed to make you feel more confident and powerful. By assuming certain postures, you can signal your mind that you feel confident, in control, and ready to face any challenge that comes your way.

Perhaps the most popular poses of all are the wonder woman poses. It is a strong body position where you stand with your feet apart, head lifted high and your back straight, and your hands placed on your hips. You might wonder whether these positions work, and if so, how they work.

Amy Cuddy has been accredited with the popularization of power posing. Power posing can greatly influence your state of mind as well as your behavior. By assuming certain strong and confident poses, it tends to cause changes in hormone levels by increasing the production of testosterone while reducing cortisol, a stress-inducing hormone. Testosterone is believed to be a hormone that makes one biologically dominant, confident, assertive, and more relaxed because of the reduction in stress-causing hormones.

When you start behaving more confident by assuming these positions, you tend to feel more confident as well. By placing your body into positions which are normally associated with the idea of power and dominance, you feel all those feelings you desire. By following power posing, you are essentially faking it until you become what you desire.\Power posing certainly affects the way you feel naturally about yourself and the way you protect yourself from the rest of the world. By improving these two things, you will feel more confident about yourself and the choices that you make. Power posing affects the way others perceive you as well. Since these positions are often associated with power, control, strength, and confidence, others will also perceive you as being powerful, confident, in control, and strong. Body language and body positioning is an important aspect of non-verbal behaviors. Most of the communication that takes place is not just through words spoken by verbal communication, but it is to non-verbal communication. Body language is what non-verbal communication is all about.

Power positioning merely refers to making certain nudges or tweaks to your regular body language to make yourself feel more confident. Power posing also makes others perceive you as being more confident. Whenever you are plagued by self-doubt or worry, try power posing to dispel all these unnecessary fears and worries. Power posing creates a mind-body nudge that helps shift the flow of your emotions in a desirable direction. It allows you to avoid any psychological stumbling blocks that can halt your progress and slowly destroy your self-confidence. Even if you don't feel all-powerful and confident, power poses will help change all this. However, it doesn't happen immediately. You need to keep practicing it daily and consistently to see positive and lasting changes.

A simple pose you can practice within the comfort of your own home is the victory pose. If you have ever watched a sporting event that you love, you may have noticed the joy with which the winners jump around to celebrate their victory. Whenever an athlete wins the race, scores a goal, or experiences any other form of victory, the common physical reaction is to raise their arms high above their heads with a closed fist to celebrate their win. Well, you are essentially required to imitate these actions to make yourself feel triumphant and victorious. You don't have to use this pose when you win, but you can start reverse engineering. Start with the feeling of triumph and the feeling of happiness and slowly make your way back to the task at hand. If your mind is already thinking like a winner, then you will automatically feel more confident about whatever you are pursuing.

Now, let us move onto the simple salutation pose. In this pose, you are required to plant your feet firmly on the ground, lift your head and chest, and outstretch both of your arms upward toward the sun. It is almost like you're standing on the ground attempting to reach out to the sun with your arms stretched wide in an inviting hug. This is a power pole; you must start practicing daily to feel more confident. Hold this pose for at least 60 seconds to feel more empowered. This is something extremely freeing as well. There is something about this position that makes you feel invincible and powerful. If you start your day with this boost of energy, it will stay with you all day long.

Whenever you are talking to your boss or someone else you want to impress, then use the wonder woman pose. Start by passing a test, standing with your feet apart, and place your hands on the hips. If your boss joins you in the break room for a cup of coffee, your heartbeat might quicken, and your mind might try to think of an interesting conversation to make. If this is the situation you are in, then channel your inner superwoman by using the wonder woman pose.

If you are nervous about an interview, then use "the performer" poses to increase your confidence. It is quite similar to the salutation pose and is named in honor of Mick Jagger. Opting for a high-power pose while amid an interview can make you seem presumptive, foolish, and even downright offensive. Regardless of how powerful it makes you feel, power poses are not meant for an interview. So, before the interview, find a safe spot yourself and use this pose. You merely need to widen your stance and throw your hands up in the air. It is like the pose a performer on stage would assume to receive applause from an audience. Allow this pose to wash over your body and mind with power and confidence. Hold this pose for a minute or 2 to enable favorable hormonal reactions to take place in your body. Once the time's up, you will feel better than you did before.

Different power positions can be used according to the situation you are in. If you are in the midst of a social event or a social gathering, then another power pose you can use is the Vanna White. Use this power pose whenever you feel a little low in confidence, especially when people surround you. Keep in mind that the basic idea of power positioning is to empower you to access your internal strength, and the simplest way to do this is by taking up a little space. So, you might not be able to outstretch your arms like you did in the salutation position while presenting a business argument, but you can still incorporate certain elements from it to form a new power pose.

By stretching your arms and using subtle gestures, you can take up more space than you were doing previously. For instance, if you are in the middle of a presentation, place one hand on the whiteboard or the computer screen or anywhere else, as long as you can outstretch your arm. You can casually rest your other hand on your hips, provided it is a social setting.

Leaning slightly forward onto a desk or the back of a chair is a great power position. Use this position whenever you are presenting any ideas at your workplace or conducting any business deals. Emmy Cuddy named this pose as "the Loomer." She considered this position to be a tribute to the former United States President Lyndon B. Johnson. President Johnson was 6 '4," and he used his physical stature to project confidence and intimidate others.

Whenever you are in a business setting and you feel the need to internalize any negative emotions you are feeling, or want to exhibit power, then use this position. If you are standing, take a second to find a chair or a table nearby and place your hands on the table while leaning forward. Without coming across as overly dominant, this position helps you seem more in control. It places you in control of your audience and shows that you demand respect and power.

Another simple power pose that is subtle but works as well as any other pose is smiling. A confident smile can not only boost your energy and make you feel more comfortable, but it also makes others feel that you are confident. Smiling has the power to influence your mood and the mood of those around you.

The great thing about using power poses is that you can use them whenever you want to. Whenever you want to access your internal stores of confidence and power, opt for a specific pose. You can use power poses before going to a job interview, giving a speech, making a business presentation, having a tough conversation with your significant other, or even before an audition. If you want to do all of this, then there is another option available to you - you can perform power poses as soon as you wake up in the morning. Start your day with a couple of power poses and recharge your body and mind with the power and confidence you want to feel.

Hack #6: Speak Up

A common fear that many people share is the fear of speaking up. The inability to speak up, not just in personal situations, but even in the work environment, can prove detrimental to your growth. If you cannot speak up, then your ability to express yourself will also be hindered. The common doubts like, "What if others don't understand what I'm saying? What if people believe that I am foolish? What will happen if I fumble for words and make a fool of myself?" can silence anyone. This kind of self-doubt can creep up on you and overwhelm you if you aren't careful.

It is easy to hold on to negativity and not say anything. However, if you don't engage in conversation or don't express yourself, you are not solving any problems. No one expects you to speak perfectly or be 100% insightful all the time. It is merely about expressing yourself. Just because you are speaking up and expressing yourself, it doesn't mean you will always contradict others. If you want to become confident, then you need to find your inner voice and be comfortable with expressing yourself. If you are struggling with speaking up, then here are a couple of simple tips you can follow to become more confident.

Start identifying all the situations where you feel comfortable expressing yourself. It could be a personal opinion, emotions, or even feelings. Maybe the situations include ones where you are comfortable with those around you - in the company of your friends, loved ones, family members, or a couple of colleagues. Once you identify a specific situation, ask yourself what is different from that situation and the other one where you struggle to speak. Now think back to how the situation was a year ago. Maybe you were not friends with the people you are friends with right now, and perhaps you were hesitant. So, what changed? When you identify the answer, it becomes easier to start expressing yourself.

If you are afraid of expressing yourself or speaking up in front of a crowd, then take small steps. Maybe you can talk to someone you trust and ask them for their opinion about your ideas. Before you commit to sharing your idea during a meeting, talk to a trusted colleague about them. After this, it becomes easier to share your opinions with no hesitation. If you want to work on improving your confidence levels, then ask for feedback. Ensure that you keep an open mind to whatever feedback you receive. It isn't always going to be positive, and whatever criticism you obtain, take it in your stride and work on improving yourself.

If you want to grow in life, you will need to step outside your comfort zone. To step outside your comfort zone, you will need a little confidence. Work on developing your ability to speak up in a lower risk environment or in a place where you know you have a support system. It could be in the form of a trusted friend, mentor, or even a colleague.

If you do have something important to say and you are hesitating, then write down the things you wish to share. If you are struggling to speak up, you can minimize the chances of stumbling, stuttering, and fumbling for words by making a note of the things you wish to share. It is okay to read out your thoughts, and it doesn't have any negative connotations. If you can express yourself clearly and concisely, then there is no harm in writing down your thoughts and sharing them. Once you write, you get a better perspective of the things you wish to share.

All opinions matter. Regardless of whether they are big or small. You don't have to hold yourself back and wait for the major issues before you start speaking up. You don't have to doubt whether what you are sharing is worth it. Try to understand yourself, but it is important to express yourself. Once you understand the reasons you are supposed to speak up, it becomes easier to share. It also gives you an internal sense of confidence to express yourself clearly and with no hesitation.

Another simple step you can use is to visualize the conversation before it takes place. Maybe you can stand in front of a mirror and practice how you want to speak up. You can concentrate on your body language, the tone of voice you use, and facial expressions while doing this. Before diving in, start visualizing the conversation of the meeting. After you have done this, it becomes easier to articulate your views. This kind of rehearsal comes in handy, and with a little practice, you will see a positive change in the way you can speak up.

If you ever hesitate to voice your opinions, then there are two simple ways in which you can frame your statements. Start by using, "this is why," or "this is what I think." By using these phrases, you will feel more prepared, and confident while expressing yourself. Apart from this, these kinds of comments help further the conversation and attract comments from others.

If you are trying to make a convincing argument or want to get your audience to listen to you, then it is not just about presenting emotions, it is about facts too. Emotions play a big part in this, but facts are equally important. When you share facts or statistics, it makes you sound more confident. Don't allow your emotions to overwhelm you whenever you are speaking out. Regardless of how deeply you feel about a specific topic or an issue, stay rational and don't allow emotions to get the better of you. If you are easily overwhelmed, then take a moment to gather your thoughts, recompose yourself, and then express yourself.

Start using the "act as if" technique discussed in the previous sections to seem more confident. If you want to change yourself, then ensure that you are willing to commit to change yourself consciously. It is not an easy process, but your efforts will pay off eventually. If you are trying to improve your confidence, then try imitating the behavior of someone you admire. If you admire the way your boss always seems confident while expressing himself, then why not try copying his body language? If you admire your parent, friend, colleague, or someone else, then ask yourself what this person would do if he or she was in the same situation that you are in? The answer to this question will give you a plan of action about how you can start speaking up.

A common problem that prevents many people from sharing their beliefs or opinions is that they concentrate too much on the outcome. If you want your voice to be heard, then you need to let go of the sphere. Stop worrying about outcomes to the extent that you forget to live in the moment. If you start sharing and speaking up, it becomes easier to gauge what the outcome will be. Instead of worrying about the outcome, start living in the moment. Regardless of the response you get from others, it is worth speaking out. For instance, if you're worried that you will be criticized for speaking up, then ask yourself what is the worst that others can do? Apart from dealing with criticism, there won't be much else, right? Once you take away the fear of the outcome, it becomes easier to start speaking up.

It is not just your verbal language, but the non-verbal language matters too. Pay attention to your body language, the tone of your voice, the gestures you use, and your facial expressions. These things speak louder than any words you speak. The simplest way to pay attention to all this is by recording yourself. Have an imaginary conversation in front of the camera and look at all the different aspects of your non-verbal communication. Maybe your posture is too dominating, or the tone of voice you use is meek. As and when you notice certain aspects you are supposed to change, start working on improving yourself.

It is not just about speaking up, but you must also be a good listener. Many people talk, but seldom do others listen. If you want to be heard, then they will listen. Notice any behavioral patterns or the style of speaking used by others. It gives you a better idea to understand how or what you're supposed to say. If you think you cannot express yourself in a crowd, then you can seek a one-on-one meeting later. By using your insights from the previous meeting, you can easily get through a personal meeting.

If you notice that someone else is having a tough time to express their opinions, then learn to be an advocate for them. If you notice that someone keeps raising their hand to express an opinion, but gets overlooked, then maybe you can say something like, "I think ___ has something she wants to share." Start speaking up for those who have a tough time expressing yourself. When you help others, it makes you feel more confident.

Once you express yourself, your confidence levels will increase. When you start asserting yourself and hold your ground, it will improve your self-confidence. If you keep doing this at your workplace, you will come across as being an assertive leader.

Hack #7: Love Yourself

Self-esteem and self-confidence are closely related to self-love. Self-love is about taking care of yourself and loving yourself unconditionally. The way you perceive yourself influences the way others perceive you. If you don't feel confident, others will not think of you as a confident woman. Self-confidence stems from self-love. Understand that you deserve to be loved and cherished not just by others, but by yourself. If you don't approve of yourself, you can never be truly confident. You need to understand your self-worth. It is easy to criticize and judge yourself and loving yourself can be difficult. Loving yourself despite all your flaws takes a conscious effort. Once you love yourself, you will see a positive shift in your level of self-confidence. Once you believe in yourself, you can take risks, be spontaneous, and engage in experiences that teach you more about yourself. Take control of your self-confidence by showing yourself the love and compassion you usually show others.

We all tend to have a specific mental picture of ourselves. This self-perception tends to influence your confidence too. Keep in mind that this picture changes based on the different life experiences you have. If this self-image you have is rather negative, then work on making it more positive. Think about ways in which you can develop yourself to fix this mental self-image.

When you start taking care of your physical appearance, you will feel more confident about yourself. Getting regular haircuts, showering daily, and maintaining general hygiene will make you feel good. For instance, don't you feel good after soaking in the tub for a while after a tiring day? If you do this daily, you will start to feel better.

Pay attention to the clothes you wear. Dress appropriately and dress in a way that enhances your best features. When you dress nicely, you will feel better about yourself, and it will make you feel more confident. Dressing nicely doesn't mean that you must splurge on a new wardrobe. It merely means you need to wear clothes that look good on you. If you want others to take you seriously, then get out of those sweaty pajamas and dress stylishly.

Internal self-talk never really takes a break unless you are asleep. Self-talk is the internal dialogue that keeps going on in your head. This self-talk can be quite damaging when it turns negative. For instance, you might be doing the laundry, then suddenly your mind might tell you it is too difficult and to take a break. Your self-talk can either motivate you or reduce your morale. The great thing is that you are the narrator of this internal dialogue. You can script it any way that you deem fit, and no one can change it. If you think it is taking on a negative hue, fill it with positivity.

If your internal critic keeps telling you that you are not good enough, or that something is too difficult, or that you don't have the skills to get things done, it is time to shut down this kind of self-talk. To do this, you need to pay conscious attention to the thoughts you think. Whenever you notice a negative thought, replace it with a positive one. If you feel like you cannot get something done, then tell yourself you need a while longer than you thought you did. If something seems impossible, tell yourself that it is impossible right now and not forever. You can improve your self-confidence by merely tweaking the way you talk to yourself.

It is not just about thinking positive thoughts, but you need to act on these thoughts as well. Your thoughts will not amount to anything unless you take action. Action is an important step to develop self-confidence. When you start acting on your thoughts, it becomes easier to feel more confident. Instead of telling yourself that you cannot do something, take the first step and challenge your inner beliefs about your abilities and yourself. For instance, if you wish to run a marathon, won't be able to do this overnight. In this case, your mind might tell you that you don't have what it takes to complete a marathon. You can challenge this belief by exercising daily. Within a month, your negative self-talk will reduce.

A common tactic used by great generals in a battlefield is that they thoroughly understand the enemy. If you don't know your enemy, then you cannot defeat him. Are you wondering who your enemy is? Well, you are your worst enemy. You are your worst critic. If you don't keep a check on yourself, you will become critical of everything you do and think. If you are trying to replace a negative self-image with something more positive, then you need to know yourself. Don't ignore your thoughts. Instead, start paying attention to them. Learn to understand why you think the way you think. Once you analyze the reasons, it becomes easier to keep a check on all sorts of negativity. If there are any limitations you have imposed on yourself, then try to see the bigger picture as to why you have these limitations. By understanding yourself inside and out, you can become more confident.

Learn to be kind and generous. Not just toward others, but yourself. If your friend were going through a nasty breakup, how would you deal with her? Would you be compassionate and offer some rational advice? Why don't you extend this compassion toward yourself? Not just others, even you deserve a little compassion. Your self-image will improve when you start being as kind and generous with yourself as you are with others.

The way you speak influences the way others perceive you. Someone in authority always speaks slowly and clearly. It shows confidence. Concentrate on the way you speak to others. If you are always in a rush, it often stems from the belief that whatever you are saying is not worthy of being heard or that you don't have the confidence to express yourself more clearly. Even if you don't feel confident initially, with a little practice, it will come to you naturally. It will make you feel more confident.

If you don't think you'll be able to do something well or excel at something, your confidence takes a beating. To get over this fear, start preparing yourself. You would not go unprepared for a major exam, would you? Likewise, learn to be more prepared for everything that life throws at you. If you are learning a new skill, you might not be confident in your abilities. However, if you practice and keep learning, your confidence levels will improve.

What are your core beliefs or the primary principles upon which you want to lead your life? If you don't want to feel directionless as you wade through the waters of life, you need certain principles. A simple example of a principle would be "to live my life according to my passions," or "I want to learn something new daily." Once you have these basic beliefs in place, it becomes easier to concentrate on any goals you have. All this will make you feel more confident.

Start setting small goals for yourself and work on attaining them. These goals can be related to your personal or professional life. It doesn't matter, as long as you attain your goals. Whenever you feel low on confidence, you will feel better by merely looking at all the goals you have attained. Most of us tend to forget about the small stuff because we concentrate only on the bigger picture. To attain a major life goal, you need to get through various small goals. For instance, if you are trying to lose weight, then a small goal could be to exercise regularly for ten days. Once you attain this goal, it will give you the confidence and motivation required to work towards attaining your big goal.

Another simple aspect of self-love is to learn to be grateful. Learn to be grateful for all the good that you have in your life. Learn to be grateful for every experience you had because it has contributed to your growth. Even if you don't see it immediately, there are plenty of things you have in your life that make you happy. It could be something as simple as having a loving family or a job you enjoy. You probably have things today you did not have a couple of years ago, and you wished for them. Now that you have these things, why don't you be grateful for them? Instead of concentrating on all the things you don't have, concentrate on the good that you do have. When you learn to be grateful for everything you have in your life, for all the things that others have given you, it helps improve your self-image.

We all tend to procrastinate from time to time. Even successful people do this. Take a couple of minutes and think about a specific task or activity you have been procrastinating for a while now. Start making a list of all the things you wish to do but didn't get around to doing them until now. Once you have a list in place, start working on them. As and when you complete an activity, strike it off your list. Whenever you complete something you have been putting off, you will feel better about yourself. It will give you the confidence you require to keep going.

Whenever you have to complete an overwhelming task or project, it can be quite intimidating. It can overwhelm the best of us. Instead of worrying about an overwhelming activity, try breaking it up into smaller, manageable chunks. It becomes easier to complete a task. When a task is perfectly manageable and attainable, completing it is easier. By completing a series of small tasks, you can attain your goal. Apart from this, whenever you complete a small task, it will improve your self-confidence. Your little achievements will soon add up. When you see that you can complete any task, it will boost your motivation too.

Chapter Seven: Confidence in the Workplace

It is difficult to be a woman in a world that's dominated by men. It is even more difficult to be a confident woman in the workplace. Even though we live in the modern world, society still burdens women with ridiculous expectations as if we were still in the dark ages. A common issue that plagues a lot of women is a lack of confidence in the workplace. Most of us worry that we're not good enough or that there is someone who is better than us. If you want to be more confident in your workplace, then here are some tips that you can start following today.

Work with The Team

Try to integrate yourself within the team at work and don't be afraid to speak up. Make an effort to get to know your colleagues, clients, bosses, or anyone else you need to work with. Try to show that you are interested and open to socializing without coming across as being too pushy. Once others know that you are not a tough person to talk to, they will start reaching out to you. It is quintessential that you work on networking with others and create business relationships. The more you understand about your work environment, the more confident you will feel.

Contribute Strategically

Whenever you work on a specific project, make it a point to actively align your workload and priorities with that of your manager or boss. Think about it from your boss's perspective - what is the most valuable thing that you can do for your boss? It might be tempting to work on projects that are not as important, but it is imperative that you make yourself a valuable asset for your team. When your approach to work is based on the idea to add as much value as you can, the results will also be more valuable, and your work will be more appreciated. If you don't contribute any value, then others will quickly forget about you. Feeling like you are a real member of a team will improve your self-confidence.

Use the Progress Principle

Teresa Amabile, a researcher at Harvard Business School, created the Progress Principle. This principle essentially states that you need to celebrate all the little wins that happened to you in order to have a positive work-life. Once you start tracking your progress and celebrate the progress you make, regardless of whether it is big or small, your productivity will improve. Not just that, but it will also improve your confidence levels. It is easy to keep track of all the work you do. You can use a journal or even an app to keep track of all the tasks you accomplish daily. Once you see the progress you make, your confidence will grow. It is not just about making progress, but you must also learn to appreciate the progress you make. It will make you feel like a valuable asset to your team.

Whenever you feel a little low on confidence, you can go through the progress journal and remind yourself of all that you have accomplished. When you see that you have come a long way from where you started, you will automatically feel better. It tends to create an internal sense of motivation that will fuel your desire to keep growing.

Avoid Comparison

Instead of worrying about what others say and do, concentrate all your energy only on yourself. Nothing can kill your self-confidence as quickly as a comparison does. Keep in mind that every individual is unique, and no two humans are alike. If you keep comparing yourself to others, you are merely wasting your time and energy. These are two precious resources that will not come back once wasted. Everyone is good at something. Instead of worrying about things you are not good at, concentrate on the things that you can excel at. If you feel you lack in a specific area, you can always work on improving your skill set. Keep in mind that it is not the end of the line. The work that you do is meaningful, and you were chosen for your position based on certain qualifications you have. So, never, not even for a second, believe that you are not worthy of the job you do.

Speaking Up

Another thing a lot of women worry about is that others will think they sound stupid. It is a major reason why a lot of people fail, because they believe their ideas aren't worth being expressed or shared. If you think you have a good idea, then speak up and express yourself. If you're hesitant to talk in front of a group, you can always seek a coworker's or trusted friend's opinion about the idea. If you want to be successful at work, make it a habit to share your ideas. Even if others think they are stupid, someone might find your ideas brilliant.

Asking Questions

This point is similar to the previous one. It is not just about sharing your ideas, but don't be afraid to ask questions either. If you don't understand something, ask for an explanation. If you don't know something, then get someone to explain it to you. It doesn't make you stupid to ask questions. Asking questions is the only way in which you can test understanding of a topic. When you understand something, only then will you be able to question your beliefs. Asking questions is a part of the process of learning. Even if others laugh at your questions, don't worry. The joke is on them and not you.

Being Bossy

A lot of women, especially the ones who are higher up the corporate ladder or hold managerial positions, tend to be wary of sharing their opinions. If you are holding yourself back because you're worried you will come across as being bossy by sharing your opinions, then think again. If you don't speak up and keep everything to yourself, others will never know your potential. Apart from this, keep in mind that you are the boss. It is okay to be nice to others. At the same time, you must not forget that you shouldn't be a pushover. Don't allow others to walk all over you. Keep in mind that you have earned your job based on your potential and merit. If your job requires you to supervise others, then do it properly. You don't have to be best friends with everyone you come across in the course of your job. A job is a job, and it is your responsibility to do it well. At times you will need to make certain tough decisions, and it might not sit well with others. All this is part of life. The sooner you make peace with all this, the better you will feel.

Dress Accordingly

The clothes you wear must reflect your confidence. According to your job description, wear clothes that suit your role and responsibility. Don't dress too casually and don't overdress either. Choose conservative clothing whenever it comes to a professional work environment. The clothes you wear must make others take note of you and regard you as a serious professional. Your clothes must convey that you mean business, and nothing else. Avoid wearing flashy and over-the-top outfits. Choose clothes with clean lines and opt for well-tailored jackets and pants. The idea is to opt for such clothes that make you feel comfortable and professional at the same time.

Saying No

Learning to say no is a skill that will come in handy in all aspects of your life. Your ability to say no directly stems from your self-confidence. If you aren't confident, then you will not be able to say no to others. Learning to put your foot down is a great way to ensure that your personal boundaries are not being trespassed. Once you are aware of all the things that are not acceptable to you, it becomes easier to say no. Whenever you are saying no, remember that you're not saying no to the person, but to the task at hand. It means that you are aware of your priorities and understand how to prioritize effectively.

For instance, if a colleague asks you to fill in for him so he can go out and watch a football match, then you don't have to do this. If you think you cannot get on with your work and cover for him, then say no. If you are unable to prioritize your time, then you will never be able to get anything done. Stop being a pushover at work. Once others realize that they can get away with anything without worrying about consequences, they will take you for granted. If you want to be seen as a valuable member of the team, then you need to learn to say no.

Establishing Boundaries

Establish certain boundaries about your work and professional life. If you want to avoid these two aspects of your life from clashing with each other, then you need to establish certain boundaries. For instance, a simple boundary would be to avoid carrying personal baggage to work and avoid working after hours at home. It is quite a simple rule. By doing this, you will feel less burned-out and will have more time to do the things you want. If you have to balance home and work with all the work you do outside, then it is quintessential that you establish boundaries. Regardless of what you do, ensure that you get a little personal time every day. It could be anywhere between 20 minutes to an hour. During this time, concentrate only on yourself. Use this time to do anything that you love. Maybe you can read a book, take a leisurely bath, watch a TV series that you like, or maybe even exercise. Don't forget to concentrate on yourself merely because you must juggle other things in life. If you stop taking care of yourself, it will negatively affect your both personally and professionally.

General Tips

You might be familiar with the saying that you only get one chance to make a first impression, and a first impression lasts a long time. It really is a good reason why you must greet a person by looking them in the eyes and a warm smile on your face. You can project self-confidence by making eye contact and by smiling. Apart from this, your posture, gestures, and the way you carry yourself tells others how confident you are as a person. One of the most effective ways of communicating your sense of confidence to others is through your body language.

Learn to accept all compliments willingly. You don't have to hide your expression of joy from others. Instead of brushing away any compliments, learn to accept them graciously. Giving is an important part of life, but so is receiving. When you receive a compliment willingly and graciously, you show others that you are confident about yourself and are aware of yourself.

Whenever you meet someone for the first time, regardless of having a conversation over the phone or in person, always give your name. When you lead by introducing yourself, it shows you respect yourself and that they should pay attention to whatever you have to say.

Being aware of yourself and your skills is not the same as self-promotion. So, don't brag. Whenever you brag, it shows you are not confident of yourself and are also seeking external approval. A confident person is quite modest. Bragging is also a sign for seeking attention, and the ones who indulge in it use it only because of their low self-worth. Every once in a while, an individual's self-confidence can take a nosedive. If you keep thinking about your difficulties in life or past disappointments, you will only make things worse. The best way to remove any doubt is to increase positive action in your life.

Whenever your self-confidence takes a beating, you don't have to overanalyze the situation. Instead, try to do something about it. When you are engaged in work, don't dwell on unnecessary thoughts, and instead focus on coming up with solutions. You might not be able to solve your problem immediately, but the more sense you try to make of it, the easier it will be to tackle the problem.

Whenever you face a challenge or a setback, think of it as an opportunity to learn rather than a failure. When you do this, your general outlook towards life will be more positive. No one is perfect, and everyone has endured failure at some point or another. It does not reflect poorly on your capacity to perform. Therefore, there is no point in allowing it to shatter your confidence. Whenever you feel you are losing perspective, you merely need to regather your thoughts. Take a break from the situation and try to remove yourself physically from the circumstances. By doing this, you will start to feel better.

By following the simple tips discussed in this section, you will become more assertive and confident at work. In fact, most of these steps are applicable to your life in general. During the initial period, you will need to implement these steps consciously. However, after a while, they will come naturally to you. Even if you don't feel confident right now, once you practice these tips, you will feel confident. You cannot become confident overnight. But with a little practice, patience, consistency, and self-care, you can improve your confidence levels.

Chapter Eight: Dating Confidence Hacks

Confidence is perhaps the most desirable and irresistible trait when it comes to dating. It's not just about looking attractive in dating, but it is about having self-confidence. When you are self-confident, it shows others that you know what you want and is not afraid to get it. Everyone wants to date someone who has confidence and has a strong sense of self-worth. A confident person looks approachable, is happy, and walks with a sense of determination. Nothing can replace confidence and learning to be confident is quintessential in every aspect of your life. The great thing about confidence is that it is not based on luck, anyone can develop self-confidence.

A confident person never feels like they are missing out on anything in life. They don't get caught up worrying about the things that can go wrong or possible rejection. Instead, they concentrate on all the good that they have and the possibility of something good coming their way. They don't feel threatened easily and stay calm even in testing circumstances. In stark contrast to this, a person running low on self-confidence gets scared easily and feels anxious or threatened whenever something doesn't go their way. They worry too much about the things that can go wrong in this process; they forget to think about all the things that are going well for them.

When it comes to dating, a confident person would think, "If I don't ask him out, I will not have a date. If I do ask him out, I at least stand a chance." In contrast to this, a person with low levels of confidence takes dating quite personally. If things don't work out like they hoped they would, they blame themselves.

Clarity About Self-Worth

You don't worry about how others perceive you. Since you already know that you are good, the way you are and are lovable, you believe that the other person will also see the same. A confident woman would not worry whether or not other men like her. If you want to be confident, then try to understand that your self-worth comes from within. Your self-worth must be independent of what the guy thinks of yours. You don't have to worry about his feelings and certainly don't have to feel stressed if his feelings are unclear. Instead, you will start working on the assumption that you are worthy of being loved unconditionally.

Set and Implement Boundaries

Self-esteem and personal boundaries are interrelated. When you know your needs and wants, it becomes easier to establish certain boundaries to determine what is and isn't acceptable to you. When you are aware of these boundaries, it becomes easier to steer clear of any pressure to do something you don't want. You cannot set or implement boundaries when you don't care and respect yourself. You are the only person who has the power to determine what your needs are. You don't have to do things because it would make your potential partner happy. You don't have to change yourself to find true love.

When you don't have any boundaries or have weak boundaries, then you might start compromising too much and will eventually lose the ability to see things objectively

When you are uncertain about your wants and needs, you cannot expect your partner to know what you want. You need to be clear about yourself, your expectations, and your needs. Only then will you be able to give yourself fully to a relationship. By establishing and implementing certain personal boundaries, you can ensure that you stay true to yourself. Losing your authentic self for the sake of a relationship is never a healthy sign. The best way to avoid your self-esteem and self-confidence from taking a beating is by establishing personal boundaries.

Avoid Over Personalization

If something goes wrong, keep in mind that you are not the only one involved in the relationship. The success or failure of a relationship is based on the partners involved. Neither partner can take all the credit when things go right, and neither should take the blame if everything is flawed. A confident woman understands that it is not fully her fault if a relationship fails. With the right attitude, you will be able to dissect the relationship and understand any mistakes you make carefully. Even if you don't click with someone, rest easy knowing that there is something else in store for you. If you don't find your match immediately, it doesn't mean the end of the road. It merely means you need to look further.

When you're no longer insecure about yourself and your needs, it becomes easier to find a potential partner. Stop obsessing and overanalyzing every interaction that took place in an attempt to uncover what you did wrong. A relationship is a two-way street, and you should not be too hard on yourself.

Don't Have to Show Off

Keep in mind that a woman who is confident about her capabilities will not try to show off or talk herself up. You will not feel like doing these things because you are secure about who you are as a person. Only those who are insecure or feel they are unworthy are the ones who try to hide their insecurity by constantly bragging. If you want to seem like a confident woman while dating, avoid bragging about yourself. If your date brags about himself and keeps talking himself up, then it is a sign that he is rather insecure. Confidence doesn't come from having to praise oneself constantly. Instead, it is an internal sense of satisfaction that makes you feel good without having to talk about it. When you feel you are worthy of something, you don't have to talk to people about it. It shows in the way you think, believe, and act. Keep in mind that you don't have to sell yourself. Whenever you are out on a date, it is not a sales pitch, and all that you need to do is to be your genuine self.

Trust Your Decisions

A key to having high self-confidence is believing in yourself and trusting your ability to choose wisely. Apart from this, when you are confident you will be equipped to deal with any situation, even if it doesn't play out like you thought it would. Even when things go awry, it will come with self-confidence. Don't constantly second-guess their actions or feel conflicted about doing or saying the right thing. When you are true to your authentic self and are comfortable in your skin, then you will be able to express how you feel precisely.

On the other hand, a woman with low self-esteem will often question her judgment, will not trust gut instincts, and will be afraid of doing or saying something wrong. Because of all these fears, anxiety and self-doubt become her natural way of life. If this is how you feel, don't be afraid to keep developing your self-confidence.

Accepting Responsibility

A true sign of confidence is accepting responsibility for one's emotions and feelings. Keep in mind that you are only responsible for the way you think and feel. You are not responsible for the way your partner feels. If something makes them feel a specific way, then it is not your problem. If your date blames you for something you didn't do, you don't have to take responsibility. Relationships are about compromise, but you don't have to be the only one who keeps compromising all the time. You need to take responsibility for your acts, both good and bad. If you make any mistakes, think of them as learning opportunities to make yourself better in the future. If something didn't work, then it is not entirely your fault.

The Way It Is

A confident woman feels secure in her relationship. If you don't feel secure about yourself, your partner, or even the relationship, then what's the point? You don't necessarily need a title of some sort to confirm the relationship. If you can sustain yourself in the relationship with no external force or pressure, then it is a healthy relationship.

If your relationship is a certain way, then that's how things are. Don't expect it to be something else, or don't lull yourself into thinking that it is something else. Don't try to change yourself or your partner for the sake of the relationship. If things are meant to last, then they will. If it wasn't meant to be, then it is a learning lesson for you.

Holding On

If it looks like things are not working out, or that you are stuck in a toxic relationship, then have the strength to move on. A confident woman knows that it is not in her best interest to stay in a bad or a toxic relationship. If you value yourself and respect yourself, then you will want to be appreciated for who you are. If you don't love yourself, you cannot expect anyone else to love you. If you have a negative relationship with your inner self, then you will just keep attracting negative people in your life. Understand that people can cause damage only if you let them. If you feel like you're being treated unfairly or that the treatment doled out to you as an acceptable, then move on. Nothing is worth sacrificing your self-esteem.

Don't Need Any Reassurance

All those who have self-confidence and self-esteem know that they are lovable and are loved. They certainly don't need a guide to remind them of their self-worth. When you are insecure, you tend to constantly seek validation from external sources, and become resentful when you don't get it. You might even end up blaming your partner by saying that he makes you feel insecure or unworthy of being loved. The harder you try to please the other person, the more damage it does to your self-worth. An insecure person always seems needy, and no one likes a needy person. If you don't feel good about yourself, then there is nothing in this world that can ever make you feel better. Even if you feel good when you are reassured, it is only temporary. This feeling needs to come from within. Unless it comes from within, your life will not go anywhere that you want it to.

When it comes to finding your partner, ensure that your heart does not solely guide your decision. At times, the heart is blinded to what the mind sees. Trust your instinct, consider your rational part of the mind, and follow your heart. Once you are guided to all these three things, you are bound to make the right decision. Don't second-guess yourself. Even if there is a moment of self-doubt, try to understand why this self-doubt stems from it. Don't try to repress or suppress any emotions or feelings. Instead, work on analyzing them and understanding them. Everything that you feel defines you as a person.

Chapter Nine: Taking Care of Yourself

When you take care of yourself and your health, your overall approach toward life improves. Self-care, or caring face else, is amongst the primary ways in which you can control your overall wellbeing. When you don't take care of yourself, your overall wellness suffers in numerous ways. Your overall wellbeing is a combination of various lifestyle factors that work together to bring about a sense of overall peace, happiness, and health. Self-esteem is your ability to believe in yourself, your skills, and your ability to get things done. To assess your self-esteem, you need to concentrate on your self-worth. Your self-worth is influenced to a great extent by the degree of your health and wellness. If you are healthy, then your self-worth increases and benefits the way you perceive yourself. It also affects your wellness. If your overall outlook of yourself is rather negative, then your wellness suffers.

On the other hand, self-care is a simple term that defines the way you treat yourself. Self-esteem is more about taking care of your mental and emotional wellbeing, whereas self-care is about taking care of your physical, financial, and mental wellbeing. It could be something as small as getting a massage after a long day, or going to bed early and getting the type of rest that your body requires. Your self-care routine is what you make of it, and it is the basis for your overall health and wellbeing.

If you're not good at loving yourself, you will find it incredibly difficult to love anyone else. Apart from this, you will also find it difficult to accept love. Self-care is an ongoing journey, and it includes a variety of things. It is something you need to do daily if you want to improve the quality of your life. If you want to feel happy, self-assured, and balanced in life, then self-care must be your priority. Unless you make yourself a priority, you cannot start living the life you want. Therefore, it is safe to say that your self-esteem, self-confidence, and self-care are all associated. If you take care of yourself, you will notice a positive change in your self-confidence.

Tech Detox

We all live in a world that's dominated by technology. In fact, technology surrounds us all the time. From the moment we wake up until the moment we sleep at night, we spend a lot of time on our mobile phones, laptops, television screens, and plenty of other gadgets. Ensure that you enjoy at least an hour of tech-free time daily. Keep your phone away, forget about all the emails, and concentrate only on yourself. All these things can be attended to later, you don't have to worry about it right now. This is also a great way in which you can forget about the worries of your usual routine.

Concentrate on Your Diet

When your body gets all the nutrition it requires, the way it functions improves. If you want to improve your overall health and wellbeing, then you need to have a sound nutritional plan in place. Ensure that your daily diet consists of plenty of fresh fruits, vegetables, lean protein, dietary fiber, and at least eight glasses of water. Most of us are often in a hurry to get through our day, and we tend to eat our meals on the go. Instead, pay attention to what, when, and how much you eat. Make a conscious habit of sitting down while eating. Learn to be grateful for every meal you eat and practice mindful eating. Pay attention to the different flavors in the food you eat and thoroughly enjoy every morsel. Once you start taking care of the food you use to fuel your body, you will see a change in your physical health.

Me Time

Regardless of how hectic your daily life gets, ensure that you set certain time aside for yourself. Schedule at least an hour of "me time" into your daily routine. This is one of the simplest ways in which you can incorporate self-care into your daily regime. If one hour seems too much to you, then maybe you can settle for 15 to 20 minutes. During this period, don't concentrate on anything else except yourself. Use this time to read a book, catch up on some sleep, or maybe even write in a journal. Do whatever you want that makes you happy during this period. You can also use this for self-reflection. Simply turn off your mind and allow yourself to feel, think, and believe whatever you want.

Mindfulness

Mindfulness is steadily gaining popularity as a great means of improving one's overall wellbeing. Mindfulness is frequently used in meditation, as it merely means that you are supposed to concentrate all your mental energy on being present. If you want to deal with stress and reduce any anxiety you experience, then start practicing mindfulness. Most of us tend to spend a lot of time thinking about the past or worrying about the future. Well, your past cannot be changed, and the future cannot be fully controlled. So, what is the point in wasting your time thinking about all this? Instead, learn to concentrate on the present. Learn to live in the moment and experience your life right now. By living in the moment, you can improve your mind's ability to focus and concentrate on your goals at hand. This practice can help improve your physical and mental wellbeing.

Exercise

You need to engage in some form of physical activity. Exercise and proper nutrition are key to maintaining good health. Try to exercise as frequently as possible. If you cannot exercise daily, then maybe you can exercise thrice every week. You don't necessarily have to go to the gym to exercise. In fact, there are various fun activities that you can indulge in to exercise all the muscles in your body. Find an activity that you enjoy and start practicing it daily. It could be something as simple as going for a jog, running, biking, hiking, or even swimming. As long as you enjoy the activity, it will not feel like a chore to you. In fact, it could be a great stress buster as well. Whenever you engage in physical activity, your body produces endorphins. Endorphins are feel-good chemicals that help tackle the stress you experience.

Stop Overthinking

Once the simplest sources of stress and anxiety are overthinking. We often get stuck up on the idea that everything needs to be perfect, or else it is not good enough. Give yourself a break and stop chasing the elusive idea of perfection. Perfection is an abstract concept at best, and it doesn't exist in reality. You can try to be the best version of yourself, but it doesn't have to be perfect. Overthinking not only worsens your levels of anxiety, but it can even easily overwhelm you. For instance, when it comes to dieting, if you overthink about what to eat when to eat and how much to eat, it can lead to unnecessary anxiety. This is one of the reasons that it is better to concentrate on your goals and just complete all the tasks it takes to meet the specifics of your goal. At times, the simplest solution is just to get started. Once you take the first step, it becomes easier. When you get into the flow of doing things, the obstacles that seemed overwhelming a while ago will not seem that scary.

Professional Growth

When you start concentrating on your professional growth, you will feel good about yourself. Start setting small goals for yourself at your work and put in the effort required to attain these goals. By doing this, it becomes easier to accomplish your major goals. Whenever a goal overwhelms you, divide it into smaller and more attainable goals. By attaining these smaller goals, you will get the motivation and encouragement required to work toward attaining the major goals.

Inner Child

What were the different activities that you used to enjoy as a child? Don't allow your inner child to grow old. Instead, make it a point to reconnect with your inner child. Maybe you loved riding a bike when you were a kid. So, why don't you ride a bike now? You might even feel like a kid again. This is a great way in which you can forget about all the worries of your adult life and return to your happy childhood. Reconnecting with your inner child, you will feel recharged, revitalized, and happier than before.

Fresh Air

Make a point to spend at least 15 to 20 minutes outdoors daily. Get some fresh air and get away from the four walls of your concrete residence. Most of us are confined to our desktops and then to the four walls of our houses. Avoid doing this. Your body needs a little fresh air. It could be something as simple as going on a walk after dinner. Stop for a moment, smell the roses, appreciate the nature around you and be grateful.

Being Grateful

Take a few minutes and think about all those bits of your life that you are grateful for. It could be something big or small. Things that you are proud of, the things that make you smile, the things you enjoy, the people who mean a lot to you, and those whom you are grateful to have around yourself. You can do this anywhere you are. You can do this while at work, while working out, or even while traveling. When you start feeling sheer gratitude, it is not possible to feel any form of negative emotions like stress or anger. We all must have things that make us instantly happy. The things that make you smile, inspire you, or simply make you happy. It could be a movie, a song, a video, a specific book, or even a friend. Make sure you keep track of these things. Spend a few minutes and make this list. Keep adding on things whenever you notice that something puts a smile on your face. The next time you are feeling low, just refer to this list.

Loved Ones

The company you surround yourself has a positive effect on your overall wellbeing. When you are surrounded by people who love and support you, you will automatically feel better. Start eliminating toxic people out of your life. You don't need any form of toxicity in your life. Whenever you notice that certain people don't contribute to your growth or keep discouraging you from growing, then cut ties with such people. Even if you think you love them, if they don't add some value to your life, you don't need them. When you are surrounded by people who are ambitious, happy, and confident and wish the best for you, your spirits will lift too. So, start paying attention to the company you keep.

When you are feeling low, the last thing you would want to do is to be around other people. Resist doing this at any cost. Life is about forming relationships and connections. The ones you love can change your mood in an instant. Make sure you choose people carefully. You need people who are positive and who will bring positivity into your life. Anyone who wouldn't fit this bill is certainly not worth your while. Stay away from negative people and all forms of negativity.

Being selfless can make you happy too. Do something good for someone else. This is bound to make you feel better about yourself. It could be something as simple as just holding the door open for someone or letting someone else ahead of you in a queue. It doesn't have to be anything extravagant. The smallest of deeds can make you feel happy.

By following the tips given in this section, you can make self-care a part of your daily routine. By concentrating on your self-care, you can improve your overall sense of wellbeing and confidence. If you want to be a confident adult, then you must not ignore the importance of self-care.

Chapter Ten: Influential Women on Confidence

Having confidence is a lifelong journey full of difficulties. All famous and successful people often seem to give out vibes of self-assurance from every fiber of their being. For most people, becoming self-confident has been a process of ongoing evolution. In this chapter, let us look at famous women who managed to overcome their insecurities and increase their levels of self-confidence.

Serena Williams

In an interview, Serena Williams once said that people probably couldn't relate to her because she is strong, powerful, confident, and black. She was often criticized because her arms were not like the other girls', her legs might not look like someone else's, and her body didn't fit the societal notions of an ideal woman's body. She had plenty of criticism to deal with before she became one of the best tennis players the world has ever seen. So how did she deal with all these haters? Well, the solution was simple. She believed that if someone didn't like her, she didn't have to like them. She believes that loving yourself regardless of what others think about you is the only way we can deal with all the negativity. By not spending all her energy worrying about fitting the notions that others had in their heads, she could excel in her career.

The takeaway from Serena Williams's life lesson is to stop worrying about what society thinks and instead concentrate on improving yourself.

Michelle Obama

Michelle Obama believes that she found her voice when she was young. She isn't aware of when it happened, but she remembers the different experiences that led to it. She counts herself to be amongst the most fortunate women who discovered the voice early because she had an older brother, and she had an incredibly close relationship with her parents. She was always involved in different discussions at the dinner table and was never treated differently from her brother. So, if her father taught her brother to play a specific sport, he taught Michelle the sport too. She had a certain degree of reinforcement from the men in her life which made her confident. Apart from that, her mother always encouraged her to express her ideas freely. Michelle's parents never spoke to her like she was a kid, they instead treated her like a mini adult.

The takeaway from Michelle Obama's life lesson is to freely express oneself without having any qualms about what others will think.

Janelle Monae

The world knows Janelle Monae as a popular artist and a famous singer. In an interview, she confessed that she wasn't always as confident as she is today. She also said that she has moments when she doesn't feel confident now and then. She got tired of feeling like this. She realized that, at the end of the day, she's the only one who has to deal with herself. She grew up in a family of strong women and matriarchs who stepped up and provided for the family even when there were no men around. Being around strong and confident women inspired her to be more confident in herself.

The takeaway from Janelle Monae's life lesson is to accept the simple fact that you are the only one who can influence the way you think.

Mindy Kaling

In an interview, Mindy Kaling said that when she gets asked the same question again and again for years on end, all the words of her answer tend to lose their meaning, even for herself. While talking about confidence, people often talk about supportive parents or a strong sense of self. Apart from these obvious things, different situations shape a person. She wasn't always as confident as she seems today. Like everyone else, she too had moments of extreme self-doubt where she felt stupid, unattractive, and unskilled. When she started working on the set of The Office, she didn't have much self-confidence. Whenever Greg Daniels used to enter the room to talk to the team, she used to raise and lower her chair as a nervous tick. She stayed anxious and kept up with the habit until one of the writers of the show asked her to stop. This just shows that confidence isn't something that a select few are blessed with. It is an ongoing journey.

The takeaway from Mindy Kaling's life journey is that anyone can become confident, provided one decides to make the conscious effort required to learn and develop this skill.

Conclusion

By now you should have a clear idea of what confidence is all about, and different ways in which you can develop self-confidence. By developing your self-confidence, you can start living the life you have always wanted and become more assertive, happy, and stress-free.

Now all that's left for you to do is start implementing all the different practical tips given in this book. Initially, you will be required to make some conscious effort and work on developing these habits. Whenever you notice any negativity creeping up or notice that you are falling back into your old patterns, take a break and work on yourself. Keep in mind that you are the creator of your own beliefs and understand that you have the ultimate power to change the way you feel about yourself and the specific situation. There is more to life, provided you make an effort to change yourself. You don't have to allow any negative self-beliefs to hold you back.

Once you follow the different tips given in this book, you will see a positive change in your life within no time. A little bit of effort, a conscious commitment, and patience are all that you need to stay on the right track.

Resources

https://weheartit.com/articles/328434240-you-re-a-goddess-the-modern-mentality-on-self-esteem

https://www.youtube.com/watch?v=ivNNgdCsY7o

https://www.sciencetimes.com/articles/17703/20170801/wearing-makeup-gives-women-confidence-and-makes-them-feel-smarter.htm,

https://www.nytimes.com/roomfordebate/2013/01/02/does-makeup-hurt-self-esteem/look-your-best-feel-your-best

https://www.wikihow.com/Be-Confident-in-Your-Looks, https://blog.michaelajedinak.com/2017/09/how-to-look-good-and-feel-confident/

https://www.gabrielacruz.ca/6-steps-to-a-goddess-mindset/

https://www.psychologytoday.com/us/blog/changepower/201605/the-9-superpowers-your-smile

https://www.briantracy.com/blog/general/how-a-smile-can-affect-self-esteem-building-healthy-relationships-with-a-positive-attitude/

https://www.anewmode.com/dating-relationships/confident-people-differently-dating-relationships/4/

https://liveboldandbloom.com/10/self-confidence/lack-of-confidence

Part 2: Self-Esteem for Women

The Ultimate Self-Help Guide to Build Habits that Will Improve Your Confidence, Self-Compassion, Assertiveness, Self-Love, and Mindset

Introduction

Has your self-esteem taken a hit over the last couple of years? Perhaps you even remember back in childhood being made to feel small, and that feeling of smallness stuck. The fact is that the self-esteem of a woman is vital to her happiness. It is the backbone that she depends upon to come across to others as a complete and confident person. Is it possible to improve your sense of self-esteem? Indeed, it is, but you need to know how to do it, and that's where this book comes in handy. Years of work with women who deal with self-esteem and confidence problems have gone into writing this book, and you want to turn the page knowing that if you do, you can change your life.

Many women make the mistake of ignoring this aspect of their lives, yet it can make the difference between happiness and unhappiness in a huge way. It can also make a difference in the way that others approach you as a woman. Have you ever wondered why some women get teamed up with losers? What about those that get into abusive marriages? It isn't a coincidence that most of these women have emotional problems brought about by self-esteem issues. Is it their fault? Not at all. It's simply that they have not yet discovered ways in which to help their self-esteem levels to rise. In fact, if you want a backup of the importance of self-esteem, you need to look no further than the psychological theory diagram that was made in the

'40s by Abraham Maslow. What he said is still relevant; he gave a list of things that people need within their lives to be happy and to make the most of their lives. One of the items on this list is self-esteem and the appreciation of others, while the uppermost item on the list is self-actualization. What does this mean? It means what's on the label! It means making the most of who you are as a woman who is very happy with her life, knowing it's going in the direction she intended.

This book was written and designed specifically for women. The advice and tips that are contained within it will help you to move out of that zone of discomfort into a better place so that you can face the world with your head held high, knowing that you maximize your life and are happy with the results of your efforts. Self-confidence and self-esteem are never far behind when you can do this. Even though you may have self-doubts at this moment, while you are reading the introduction, the chapters within this book will certainly take you where you want to go. Your life lies out ahead of you. There's a child inside you. There's also a goddess, waiting for you to recognize her needs. Once you do, you will surprise yourself because your potential stretches much further into the horizon than you may imagine. Take this journey and know that you are not on your own. There are others with you every step of the way, and reinforcement comes in that nod of approval you give yourself in the morning as you start your day. It also comes from what you get back from life when you put your best foot forward. People around you will notice the butterfly that is emerging and will want to share that victory with you.

Lastly, in this introduction, I will tell you a secret. Your life is only beginning. If you thought that you would have to hide behind damaged self-esteem forever, then the book will prove to you how wrong that perception is. You have so much power to change your life and to become the woman you always wanted to be. Let the book be your guide to self-realization as the woman you were always intended to become awaits. There is no time like now to take that leap of faith.

That's where this book comes into play. The books deal with the problem of self-esteem from a woman's perspective and help readers to perform exercises and activities that will help them to build themselves back up again. Stop being a victim to life and start taking your life to another level. This book will help you to do just that. You may be surprised at the determination and courage that is hiding within you.

Chapter One: Self-Esteem Psychology 101

"We use language to create realities. Use it to create a version of you that you love." –Mariella Dabbah

What makes a woman suffer from self-esteem issues? Well, contrary to what you may find on some websites, women don't automatically suffer from this in adolescence. They may go through it as they grow, but it's not simply something that happens because a girl is growing up. Some girls grow up with a super sense of identity and never experience self-esteem issues at all. They fly through their lives and find happiness is very easy to achieve, while others struggle. Others may have an over-the-top level of self-esteem that you could call uber-ego, and that's not healthy. Let's have a look at some major signs of self-esteem issues that you can go through as a checklist to see whether what you believe you are suffering from is actually self-esteem related:

☐ You feel pessimistic and don't expect good things to happen to you

☐ You crave approval from other people

☐ You feel you are unworthy of other people's love

☐ You don't like yourself very much

☐ You tend to self-sabotage and never really follow through

☐ You may blame others for your misfortunes

☐ You may seek sympathy and occasionally act the drama queen

☐ You may not look after yourself as well as you should

☐ You may seek your security in other people

☐ You may be lazy when it comes to making friendships

☐ You may be a bit of a pushover when it comes to being used by others

If you can relate to any of these, then perhaps you need to look further, and this book will explain what's happening when any of these are applicable in your case. Each girl is born with the same amount of self-esteem. However, what happens in your life and how you relate to others around you will dictate how you respond to life and how much self-esteem you retain. Self-esteem can be mended if, for example, you find that you suffer from any of the above symptoms. It's simply a case of following the habits shown in a later chapter. For now, write down which of these you believe applies to you because you are currently making yourself aware of a problem, and that's a good thing. Once you admit the problem, solving it becomes easier and less painful.

Think of this 101 as your introduction to self-esteem issues and understand that just because you suffer from one or more of the above symptoms doesn't mean you are past redemption or that you can't do anything to change any one of them. You can, but it will take a little work on your part to put these things right so that you face the world on equal terms. It's a great feeling when you know that you don't have to measure up to other people's standards and that you can simply be you. This has always been the case, but as stated earlier, your experiences through the course of your life dictate how you respond to life and can be the underlying causes of self-esteem issues.

You may not have been loved in the way that you hoped, or perhaps you didn't love yourself. Regardless of this, the symptoms apply to you in one way or another, or you would not have been browsing books on Amazon trying to find solutions.

☐ You feel pessimistic and don't expect good things to happen to you

In the case of feeling like this, perhaps you are accustomed to things going wrong. Here you can use the example of someone who has been made to believe that they are clumsy. They will believe that they are clumsy, and as a result, will find that their approach to life actually makes them clumsier than someone who does not believe themselves to be clumsy. Self-esteem works on experiences, and if you feel pessimistic, perhaps it's because you are approaching life with a bleak view because of experiences that you have been through in your life. Perhaps you suffered from parental disapproval, or you failed your exams. Perhaps you have failed relationships in your past and expect nothing short of a disappointment, which is what feeds your pessimism. The other reason why people use pessimism is as a shield. If you don't expect anything, then you can't be disappointed. However, as far as self-esteem goes, this approach is self-defeating. You do need to believe in yourself, and so pessimism isn't an option.

You may suffer from a pessimistic attitude because of other things. Perhaps you were brought up to expect nothing, but now you are an adult, and there are many things that you should expect as standard to your life. These words are important, so make a note of them. You should expect RESPECT FROM OTHERS, RESPECT FROM YOURSELF, and THE CHOICE IN LIFE TO AGREE OR DISAGREE when people want you to accept things that you question in your mind. The fact is that although someone else may be more knowledgeable than you, no one has the right to dictate the life that you live, and you will find out that the only person holding you back in this respect is you. Perhaps you lack the assertiveness actually to speak your mind, but that's okay too. We will show you how to deal with this throughout the chapters in the book. You must read it all, rather than jumping forward to find solutions, because the better your understanding of self-esteem, the more likely you are to understand the solutions being offered in a later chapter.

☐ You crave approval from other people:

This is more common than you may think. When you don't have confidence in yourself, you tend to look elsewhere for it. People with self-esteem issues do this because it makes them feel validated. However, they have not yet learned to validate themselves so that they don't need external validation. This is a bad habit that doesn't feed self-esteem at all. You may think that asking your boss if you did a good job will give you positive feedback, but you will already know you did a good job, so why do you need his validation? People who crave this kind of attention have problems finding the validation they need within themselves. There are some exercises later in the book that will help you to deal with this and to learn to approve of yourself above all else because that approval is your steppingstone to confidence. The validation that you get from others is momentary, and the feeling of achievement does not last. Only when you validate yourself does it become part of who you are and go with you through your life. You are an individual and should need no validation from anyone else at all. You should know your saving graces as well as your potential errors, but many people go through their lives seeking validation because they don't believe that self-validation works. It does, and it works better and longer-term to help you to overcome self-esteem issues.

☐ You feel you are unworthy of other people's love:

This can quite regularly stem from feeling unloved by people you trusted to love you. It may be that you believe yourself unworthy of love because people you love seem to be treating you in that way. Thus, it must be so. However, although relationships that are not positive can lead to self-esteem issues of this kind, they don't have to. You have to learn self-love, and that's a tough lesson for someone to learn when they are beginning to deal with self-esteem. Don't be concerned. This book will show you how self-love happens and how you can work toward it. This area of the book also deals with people who don't like themselves very much because they lack self-love. You may be the woman that sits in the corner at parties, not expecting anything to happen. You may be the person who doesn't even go to parties because you feel out of your depth in a social environment. However, you haven't yet learned to unleash the goddess inside you, and we will also discuss this later in the book. No one is unworthy of love. If you believe that, then it makes the world a potentially bleak place. Remember, even the people who make bad choices were loved at some stage in their lives. Whatever you have done in life and whatever you have had done to your emotions, this is fixable, but you need to learn to let go and move forward.

☐ You tend to self-sabotage and never really follow through:

A lot of people who don't follow through do this because they are afraid of disappointing themselves and others. The lack of confidence comes from a lack of self-esteem and can be looked at from another angle. What would be the worst-case scenario if you failed? Do you have to be good at everything? The fact of the matter is that there are things you can be good at and with which you can follow through. You just haven't found them yet. The other way to look at this is that you may just be afraid of success. That may sound a little weird, but when a singer brings out a wonderful record and never produces anything like it again, it can spell the end of their career. Similarly, people are afraid to take that first step because it's hard enough, and they don't know if they can keep to that high standard that people will expect of them. In the case of a promotion, some women sit back and avoid it because they don't want to be made to look foolish by not being able to live up to others' expectations. Look at situations in your life and ask yourself what stopped you from succeeding, and it's almost certain that your approach had something to do with that failure-based attitude.

☐ You may blame others for your misfortunes:

In this case, you blame others because it's easier than facing up to the fact that you didn't do the things in your life that you wish you had done. The fact is that a lack of self-esteem can hold you back, and sometimes it's easier to point the finger at someone else than it is to stop and examine your actions. I once knew a relative who did this all of her life. She was exceptionally talented, but instead of going on the stage and becoming a well-known concert pianist, she used other people as her excuse for not doing it. "My mother never really encouraged me", was one of the excuses. "I had to go out and get a paying job", was another excuse. All the time, she felt resentment because she had failed to live her dream, but never really saw herself as her own stumbling block. It was easier to blame the birth of her children or the attitude of her husband than it was to look to her own personal failure to let her inner self shine. Her self-esteem was low, and it was this that made her so thoroughly unpleasant to people around her, while she could have taken to the stage and would have indeed enjoyed a very worthwhile career had she made that choice. At the end of the day, blaming others for your misfortunes doesn't help you to get beyond them. It is your reaction to circumstances that will generally affect you if you have self-esteem issues.

☐ You may seek sympathy and occasionally act the drama queen:

There's a big problem with this one. I have dealt professionally with people who have suffered from this, and at the time of playing the drama queen, they were not really aware that they were doing this. The reason why women do this is to draw attention away from the real problem. Don't worry if you have been guilty of this. Many women do this in an attempt to gain attention, and although they don't know their motives, they are usually pretty innocent ones. They do not use drama for the sake of manipulation. They simply use it because their lack of self-esteem wants to make them look more important in the eyes of the world that is seemingly ignoring them. The young girl who runs away may not hate home but may just be trying to be noticed amid a growing family. A girl who wears black lipstick and goes Goth isn't doing it to annoy people. She is doing it because she is trying to find her own style and personality, but not looking inward at who she really is. Self-esteem won't be earned in this way. It simply twists the thoughts in your mind even more than they are now, and honestly facing up to who you are is the first step toward self-realization and love.

☐ You may not look after yourself as well as you should:

Do you know why women do this? Within their heart and soul, they believe that they should give their attention to others more than thinking about themselves. To a certain extent, it's endearing because other people feel that these are very caring people. But if you stop caring for yourself, eventually it catches up with you, either in the form of stress or anxiety, and you will reach a point where you need to look after yourself more than you do others. You were not born to be a martyr, to give up on important things for the sake of others. There's being kind, and there's being neglectful, and when you are kind and look after yourself correctly, then you will find that the mix is a far healthier one for not only you but the people around you. Imagine going into a relationship while being someone YOU consider as incomplete or not worthy of looking after. Does that mean that your partner is obliged to do all those things for you? The point here is that to help build up your self-esteem, you don't need the approval of others, but you do need your self-approval, and this will be more likely to follow if you respect yourself and look after yourself as you should. Anything less than that, and you are offering a relationship a partly built person instead of a fully developed and capable person.

☐ You may seek your security in other people:

This point, as well as the last two, is all about becoming someone else's doormat. You please people because you don't know how to please yourself and have not yet gained the confidence to say "no." You feel incomplete without a partner in life and try not to spend too much time alone. You feel that you are part of a relationship but that without the other part, you cannot continue. However, this is something that you do need to address, and we will show you how. The problem with this manner of thinking is that it leaves you open to being abused by people around you who will take advantage of the fact that you need them more than they appear to need you. When you can even out the odds, you will find more people need you for all the right reasons, and you can leave those who use you behind. You will also find that your own company is not as frightening as you first thought. When you find self-love, your own company is often enough, and even when you are in a loving relationship, you don't feel frightened of being alone. You appreciate that you and your partner are both WHOLE people without needing someone else to support them, though you do appreciate the love that you get from a partner who is also WHOLE.

The book will lead you through these dilemmas and show you how to deal with them as well as help you to find your best self so that you never need to worry about self-esteem again. Do I expect you to have any doubts? Of course. Everyone is entitled to doubt something from time to time, but if the core of your being is solid, then the doubts are overcome easier and don't become the focus of your life. That's the difference between a woman with self-esteem and one who has none. Don't worry, if you have read this far, you have miles to go, but the book will tell you how to do all these things, and you won't be completely on your own while you work toward the transition from a woman with self-esteem issues to one who is confident in herself and her abilities, her beliefs, and her likes and dislikes. You have a whole treat ahead of you, so turn the page and bear with me.

Self-Esteem Includes the Following Elements

- ☐ The ability to depend upon yourself
- ☐ The ability to be dependable
- ☐ The ability to try new things
- ☐ The ability to say "no" when this is your choice
- ☐ The ability to avoid clinging to people
- ☐ The ability to recognize your achievements

These are the facets that we will be working on together through the course of this book, and the whole purpose is to help you to see yourself as the whole person that you are, rather than letting self-esteem get in the way of building fruitful and enjoyable relationships with others. People with self-esteem issues can't do this because they have too many doubts. There are ways to stem those doubts, and this will also be covered within the coming chapters. If you have read this far and are beginning to recognize yourself as being someone with self-esteem issues, don't be afraid to turn the pages, as they hold a huge amount of potential for you to become that person you always wanted to be. We all have this ability, and there are no exceptions. There are no excuses and no reasons why you cannot be the star of your own life. When you become that star, you will be recognized by others for the beautiful person that you are, and that's when life starts to happen.

Chapter Two: Self-Esteem versus Self-Confidence

"When you start seeing your worth, you'll find it harder to stay around people who don't" ~ Unknown.

Self-esteem is what you think of yourself. Inflated self-esteem means that you are perhaps acting in a superior way, and this can be a problem. Low self-esteem means that you don't put enough attention into the caring equation when it comes to looking at the most important person in your life – and that's you.

Although you may be tempted to see both of these problems as being the same, they are not. Yes, there are similarities, but you can lack confidence without having a lack of self-esteem. Situational anxiety can make you feel a lack of confidence, although as soon as you are over that situation, you may not experience that lack of confidence again until another anxious moment happens. However, someone with self-esteem problems will demonstrate this in various ways.

Self-Confidence

If you have self-confidence, you are unlikely to feel uncomfortable in a social situation. You are happy in the skin you are in and carry yourself in such a way that people can clearly see that you have a grown-up head on your shoulders, and a lack of confidence does not impair your approach to life. Self-confidence is affected by what you know, and some people may feel a lack of confidence while they are learning new things. While these situations may produce self-doubts, the difference between this and a lack of self-esteem is that the doubts only usually last until that hurdle is overcome. These are signs of self-confidence:

☐ You are happy to do things on your own

☐ You are happy with your learning abilities

☐ You are happy around people and can easily fit in with new people

☐ You are happy with your place in the world

☐ You don't find it too hard to learn new things

☐ If you fail in something you do, you don't mind

☐ You like yourself in general

☐ You have friendships that are give-and-take, and understand friendship.

Self-confident people appear to be happy in their lives and are willing to try new things. They are likely to have more ambition than those with self-esteem issues and will relate to others better than those who are always looking inward at themselves as not fitting in. If you lack confidence, it's usually focused in an outward direction rather than being negatively biased against you; you will adjust to situations, and once you have adjusted, you will no longer lack confidence. It's a normal state of affairs. Imagine that you are about to meet your boyfriend's parents for the first time. You love your boyfriend, and you naturally want to make a good impression. The girl who lacks confidence will want to find it by logical means, by talking and trying to impress in a simple way. She won't doubt her abilities. She doesn't show herself to be uncomfortable but accepts that the situation may make her feel a little out of her depth. She will most likely seek the advice of her boyfriend about what she should wear, not wishing to underdress or overdress. She will simply doubt the situation until it becomes more comfortable. The person with self-esteem issues has more to worry about because the problem isn't just what those parents think of her, but that she will overreact in an attempt to correct the things that she feels are wrong with her, and that can come over in a different way that is less acceptable.

Self-Esteem

We were all born with equal self-esteem. However, it is affected by the way that people around us perceive us. We take feedback from our interactions with others, and sometimes that feedback is negative. Whereas a person who has self-confidence problems needs to overcome the hurdle of learning something new, someone who has self-esteem issues will look for validation from other people because they find no validation from within themselves. People with high self-esteem may show these traits:

- ☐ They have carefully set boundaries
- ☐ They know their capabilities
- ☐ They can trust themselves
- ☐ They can do things on their own
- ☐ They are confident and sure of themselves

Why would someone with high self-esteem need boundaries? Because they know what acceptable behavior is to them, and they will accept nothing less than that. All human beings need boundaries, although those with lower self-esteem sometimes feel that they don't have the right to create boundaries and thus show themselves to others as being easy prey. Let me explain a few obvious boundaries, and you can expand on them, so you can see why they are created, and in fact, how they are created. When you become a teen girl who is developing breasts, you may wish to have more privacy in the bathroom or the shower. That's perfectly normal and part of growing up. In the case of a child who has learned to use the potty, that child may feel that he doesn't want to wear diapers anymore because it makes him feel like a small person when he has earned the right not to wear them. This last point is a little exaggerated, as most parents will know, but the idea of showing it was to demonstrate that at all ages we create boundaries. We don't want our brothers and sisters playing with our things without permission. We learn to say, "thank you" and "please", but as an adult, you have to look at the overall picture of your life and create solid boundaries that other people respect. Typically, acceptable boundaries existing throughout your life are those such as:

☐ Don't look in my handbag. It's private.

☐ Don't use my phone without asking me first.

☐ Don't choose my clothes for me.

☐ Don't treat me like a servant.

These are all reasonable boundaries, and once the people around you accept that these represent acceptable behavior to you, then they respect them. If they don't respect them, you can complain to them that your boundaries are not being respected and expect them to apologize. We create boundaries because we all have a private bubble around us. Have you ever been on a train and had someone's coat pushing against you and taking up your space? Well, it's natural that you don't want strangers impeding upon your personal space, but it also works in the same way with boundaries. There are acceptable and unacceptable behaviors; finding out what these are and making them known helps people around you to respect you and to respect the boundaries set.

Someone with high self-esteem usually likes their own company and doesn't mind being left out of social situations. They are happy to do things on their own and feel that those who wish to be anti-social have the problem rather than it being their own problem. However, when that self-esteem is lacking, then people can use an individual to such an extent that he/she may feel like they are being treated like a doormat (but are unlikely to do anything to change that, as it's what they expect). Thus, defining boundaries becomes quite important for people who suffer from self-esteem issues, and the solutions will be discussed in future chapters. Boundaries stop things like this from happening and define your rules in life. If you don't want to babysit every Saturday night for the rest of your life, make it clear that you need some Saturdays for you. You make the rules in your life, and you do not permit others to use you in a way that is detrimental to your own personal growth.

There is a clear distinction between self-esteem and self-confidence. Although someone who lacks confidence may be shy in new situations, it's likely to be because of the unknown, whereas the person who has self-esteem issues will not want to socialize because they feel they are undeserving or don't fit in. These are two different attitudes, but both produce that feeling of inadequacy in one way or another. To get over one, you have to deal with the other. Thus, working on self-confidence can help a person to gain self-esteem, and vice versa.

Observe people for the next week and see who you would classify as being confident and who you would say has self-esteem issues. You need to focus outside of yourself sometimes to see how the world works. This isn't your solution; it's merely a tip to help you to see people for who they are so that you get a better idea of the difference between self-esteem issues and lack of confidence.

A person with confidence will not need time to answer a question. A confident woman isn't afraid of being heard. However, someone with self-esteem issues may not have the same reaction because a lot of their thought processes are inward so that they don't always make themselves aware of what is happening around them. Ask someone who has confidence in what they are good at, and they will not hesitate to tell you their passions and strong points. However, a person with self-esteem issues may struggle to find anything they can boast about, even if they are good at certain things.

Look at the way that people present themselves. This is interesting. You may have two women who dress identically, but the confident one will always shine when the two are compared. Body language comes into the picture at this stage, and you can instantly recognize confident posture as compared to the posture of someone with self-esteem issues. Look at the high heels. Does she walk proudly in them, or does she stumble because she is unsure of herself? Look at the body language. Does one woman stand straighter than another? The fact is that you don't actually have to speak to be recognized as being someone with a lack of self-esteem. The actions of your body will give it away.

Who are you? Who do you want to be? Who are you capable of being? All of these are relevant questions because they help to make you into who you show to observers in your life, and that makes a whole heap of difference to the way that you live your life and interact with others.

Look at people's smiles as well. This gives you a clue as to how confident they are. Does the smile come from true feelings of self-worth? If it does, you will know it. However, if it's a nervous smile, it can give the impression that self-esteem may be an issue. There are many kinds of smiles, so, over the next week, see if you can distinguish the differences – look for sincerity, nervousness, and insincerity. A smile can convey all of this, and you will begin to see how posture and the movement of facial features make a huge difference in how you are perceived.

"Smile, for everyone, lacks self-confidence and more than any other one thing a smile reassures them." ~ Andre Maurois

Chapter Three: Meeting Yourself – Identifying who YOU Really Are

"A good guy will tell you that you are beautiful. A real gentleman will make you believe it!" ~ Anon

Have you ever asked yourself who you are? For the sake of this exercise, I want you to sit and think about it for a moment and find all of the adjectives that you can to describe who you think you are. You know you can use whatever words you like, as no one is going to read this. It's an exercise simply to demonstrate something of which you may be unaware.

Now, look at the words that you have used to describe yourself and place them into two separate columns. One side will show all the positive things that you have to say about yourself, and the other side will list all the negative things that you said about yourself. I would bet that the negative side is longer than the positive side. That's because a large portion of all of the thoughts that we think each day is negatively biased. In the old days, when our caveman ancestors had to protect themselves from huge creatures, it was self-preserving to think negative thoughts. It kept them on their toes and made them very aware of the danger. However, those dangers don't exist today, but we still think in the same negative way, and people think this is our self-defense mechanism against getting hurt. However, it doesn't quite work in that way.

You have approximately 70,000 thoughts per day, and these conversations that go on in your head start from the moment you wake up. If you get up on the wrong side of the bed, you can have negative thoughts flood your mind all day long. It's not uncommon. Now, let's look at the list you made of all the negative things you thought about yourself. Surely, there will be a fair number of negative attributes that you put down to being you.

I want you to pick up this list, and look at the length of it, and then fold it in half and tear it into shreds. Place the paper in the bin. That's what your thoughts are worth at this moment in time. You thought them, and then they were gone. You defined yourself in words and believed that those words accurately described who you are. But have you ever thought that they are just thoughts and that they don't have any bearing on the reality of who you are? Who you are is much more complex than that, and your thoughts don't make or break you unless you let them.

Besides, the things that you think can change. Suppose I was to ask you the same thing just after you met a man whom you believe is going to become the love of your life? Your answers would be different. Suppose I asked you just after you received a letter that said that you didn't get the job you were after. The answers would once again change, but you are still the same person. In fact, every moment of your life is different, and the way you feel about yourself differs as well, which means that the value of these negative thoughts is zero. You don't improve yourself by merely looking at your thoughts unless you learn something from them.

If you have self-esteem issues, you may already think that you know who you are; even if you only have confidence problems, you probably have a vague idea of where this chapter is going. However, I want you to think in a new way, and that's the part that is not going to seem natural to you for the time being. Bear with me as you start on this new journey because I want to show you the power of thought, and your power over what those thoughts do to your mind.

How the Brain Works

To understand better, you have to understand a little more about the structure of the brain and which parts of the brain tell you to be wary when you are placed in a situation that makes you uncomfortable. It's the hippocampus area of the brain, and it records all of the things that appear important to you. It monitors your activities and looks for repetitions in your behavior because it sees those as being pretty important to you. As you grow up, you learn to say "please" and "thank you" at the appropriate times, and by now probably do that without even thinking about it because they are habits that have been recorded in the hippocampus. The hippocampus takes a lot of mental work out of your life and will do things automatically before you even have time to think about them. Thus, if you think bad things whenever you are in a situation where you need confidence, then that part of the brain will automatically switch to making you think things like:

- I am not good enough
- I can't do this
- I am clumsy
- I am not worthy

The thoughts are all coming from you. But what if the thoughts were different? Well, they can be. When you face situations with a different attitude and start to respond to social situations with positive statements, your hippocampus records those positive responses and will use these as your normal responses in the future. Just as you learned to say "please" and "thank you", you will learn to respond positively to the things that happen in your life. The thoughts are not worth anything until you start using them to reinforce who you are rather than trying to make yourself less of a person.

Begin to wonder what would happen if you treated your thought patterns differently. For example, when negative thoughts happen, imagine yourself switching the volume down so that you can no longer hear the negative words being said. Then on occasions when you see something positive about yourself, imagine turning the volume up and basking in those positive thoughts. What you are feeding to your hippocampus is the fact that you believe in yourself and are building your self-esteem and confidence.

If I was to ask you to write down the things that you like about yourself, you might not be able to think of that much. That's because you are not accustomed to doing this, and if you hang out with people who are also negative toward you, chances are they reinforce all those negative feelings that you have... but what if this could change? It can, and the way that the lady in the video above did it was to gather her clients around her and learn to accept compliments from the other people who formed that circle. You and I don't have that circle, but we do have the ability to do the same thing. If you spend time with people who are positive toward you instead of those who are negative, you gradually start to build a much different picture, simply by learning to chalk up those compliments and thank people for them. Mentally note when you get compliments, and for this exercise, I want you to go through the next week and instead of thinking about the negative things about yourself, celebrate the positive things that people say about you and the things that you find yourself thinking that are positive affirmations of who you are and what you like about yourself.

Spend Time with Supportive People that Love You for Who You Are

This is important because it's your reinforcement. When people believe in you, you begin to realize that you can't be all bad.

Otherwise, they wouldn't be in your life. Perhaps they have their motives for being there, but these are people who are willing to give and take in a relationship and who are there for you when you need someone to be. It doesn't matter how many friendships you have or whether you are the most popular girl on the block. None of that matters because one friendship that is solid and reinforcing is better than ten friendships that you cannot depend upon. Ask your friends about who they see you as, just like the lady did in the video, and explain why you are doing it beforehand. Someone else in your group of friends may even want to join in to help her to increase her confidence or self-esteem level. Make sure that they don't think that you are fishing for insincere compliments, but write up a list of questions and listen to their responses so that you get to see who you are from the point of view of people you like. Some of the questions could be the following:

- Do you see me as a nice person?
- Do you think that I am pretty?
- Do you think that I am a positive addition to your life?
- What can you tell me about the positive side of my character?
- What would you say are my strengths?

Delete the negative thoughts and boost the volume on the positive ones, and don't forget to say "thank you" for the feedback that your friends give you, whether it appears to be positive or negative. The thing is that these people are trying to help you with your insecurities, and all of their feedback has value. If you get any negative feedback, you can turn down the volume or, since these are good friends, you can examine the answers and see how you can use those answers to turn negativity into positivity. People with self-esteem issues take things far too personally, and that's because they are half expecting negative feedback but don't know what to do with it when it happens. However, if you learn what to do with constructive negative feedback, you help yourself to develop as a human being. If the negative feedback is something you can do nothing about, turn down the volume. For example, you can do nothing about your height. You can do nothing about your accent or physical traits that are built-in. Perhaps you could improve on those, but you can't change genetic physical things about yourself, so you shouldn't take negative feedback to heart. Ask yourself if it is something you need to learn from, and if there is nothing to learn, switch off the volume.

There's a practice called mindfulness, which is very useful for people who feel that they lack confidence or self-esteem. Although it wasn't invented for this purpose, it does help people to become happier and healthier. When you think something positive about yourself, boost it. Write it down in your journal. Carry a journal with you everywhere and use this to read through before you go to bed at night. This will reinforce the positive thoughts that you had about yourself that day. Perhaps you thought, "I like the shape of my nose", or "I like that I am not the same as everyone else", or anything at all that is positive. Now to deal with the negative self-image, you need to train your hippocampus to see reactions which it isn't expecting, and that's where mindfulness comes in.

When you feel negative thoughts, instead of letting them take over your feelings, switch them off. Use mindfulness to do this. It's very simple. Breathe in and count to 7 and while you are doing this, let go of the thought. Breathe out and notice things around you at this moment in time. Look at colors, smell aromas, touch something, and be in the moment, replacing negative thoughts with positive input from your feelings. It isn't the easiest thing in the world to do at first, but as I said, the hippocampus is recording your reactions, and after a while of doing something or responding differently it will automatically kick in and create a new habit; after that, it's plain sailing because once a habit is established, it takes work to get rid of it. So banishing negative self-talk and replacing it with being in the moment is a far more constructive way to deal with the negativity you feel about yourself before you go into an exam room or when you don't think you will get the job you are applying for. While breathing, hold your head up high, so breathing is made easier, and let the breath cancel out the negative thought. You can use this in moments of stress as well because this type of breathing helps you to contain panic and let go of it. Thus, you are in control of it, and once you realize this, you will find that negative thoughts don't have a lot of impact on your panic buttons anymore.

The Two-Way Mirror

Have you ever thought about what people see when they look at you? The fact is that they see an unbiased view of a human being, but what if you could give them more than that? Imagine that every person in the world goes through all the negative thought processes that you do, and learn to compliment and be kind to others. Have you ever seen what happens when you smile at someone? Usually, unless they are stressed out and in a world of their own, they smile back. A radiant smile is returned to us a thousand times a day, and it's a wonderful thought that those around us see us in such a positive light. Be kind to friends. Be supportive of friends and don't be afraid of compliments because, in this way, you are not just building up who you are, you are also improving the lives of others.

The two-way mirror effect is rather clever. If you are genuinely complimentary to someone you know, you feel good about what you said, and they feel good about it too. They also feel positively toward you, and this shows in the way that they react. That reaction comes back to you, and so it goes on until you start to see a better image of yourself emerging. Welcome to who you are. Embrace who you are and take pleasure in being that human being that makes a difference in the lives of others, and in doing so makes her own life better.

When you say thank-you for a compliment you are given, you are acknowledging it and using it to create positive thoughts in your mind.

So do others. Simply be grateful for compliments you receive and thank that person for the thought. Then pay it forward to someone else. We can't change the world that we live in without making changes in the way we perceive ourselves. When you have the confidence to tell someone that her hair looks nice or that her dress is lovely, you are doing more than that; you are spreading confidence, and that never hurt anyone. The other thing that you are doing is viewing something in a very positive way, which makes you feel good about being you. You can't fail to feel good about yourself when you are friendly to people and ask nothing in return for your compliments.

Think of the two-way mirror. You see a human being in the mirror, but the mirror is looking back at you. Others notice the way that you present yourself, so imagine the mirror from both sides so that you build up the image that others get. It's a little like a magnet for positivity, but one that doesn't include allowing yourself to be used by people when nothing is coming back. You don't need physical validation, because the validation you get comes from a happy hippo who sees you as someone who positively responds to life. The next time that you find yourself feeding the hippocampus with misery or self-doubt, just think of feeding the poor creature with positivity, so that you begin to live with a happy hippo instead of one who perpetually reminds you that you lack in some way.

Meeting yourself head-on can be a little scary, but you can get over those initial fears, start to examine the good parts of your personality, and work from there. Look after how well your hair looks, and even go as far as taking care of those toenails. Every part of this person is you, and you are now meeting yourself head-on and understanding a little more about yourself through self-examination. If you know that you neglect something, it's okay. Everyone does, but that doesn't mean you can't work to improve your image or to change your situation as time passes. The person that you meet today will be someone else tomorrow, but the underlying core will be the same. You need a stable base upon which to stand, and after that, life will become easier for you.

Look in the mirror and see yourself for the first time in all your glory. You are a wonderful human being and go far beyond what is seen on the surface. Now, you are going to start to get to know the different elements that make you who you are. This is the only way that you can change your approach and learn self-love, and indeed, self-appreciation. It doesn't mean becoming vain. It means appreciating who you are and learning that you can make the most of who you are simply by changing a couple of stray habits.

An interesting thing to note in this regard is that the social butterfly from schooldays probably isn't the most successful person in the world these days. As you grow, perspectives change, and different things come into play. I once knew someone who was terribly unpopular at school, and the other girls were relentless in their teasing of her. However, instead of turning inward and shrinking, it taught her to be compassionate and kind, and she now has a career doing exactly what she loves – looking after people who need help. Your future isn't bleak. Your lack of self-esteem doesn't spoil it. When you meet the person that you'll become when you lose your self-esteem problems, you will be very proud of that person. You will become proud of who you are and what you stand for because it's a natural follow-on from learning about your interactions with others and changing small things about yourself that matter to you.

When you meet yourself in the mirror, always be honest. Always appreciate the good things about yourself and try to do something about things you are not happy about. Remember, it's more than the surface. It's all about who you are inside, so stop trying to change things over which you have no control. The surface looks, your height, your complexion is all part of being you and are as individual as all women should be. You have attributes that others don't have. You have depth, and you have courage. How do I know that? I know that because you are still reading and still learning about how to see yourself from a neutral perspective so that you can make yourself into anyone that you want to be. This is who you are.

Chapter Four: Self-Doubt – Spot it, Silence It!

"The moment you doubt whether you can fly, you cease forever to be able to do it." – J. M. Barrie

Have there been times in your life when you were obsessed with the idea that you couldn't do something? Most of us have felt like this at some time, but when you do this more often than you have positive thoughts, this can affect self-esteem and self-confidence. If you are accustomed to saying, "I can't," you are feeding the hippo with bad food. Think of the hippocampus as a huge hippo. When you feed him, you want to feed him positive things, because when he is grouchy, you get grouchy. He remembers and will always make you respond to circumstances in life in the way that he sees as your normal way. When you tell him regularly that this isn't the way you are going to respond, you change the habit of talking to yourself negatively. You have to spot self-doubt and eradicate it. That means showing the hippo that you don't have self-doubt and that it's so insignificant when it happens that you can laugh it off and move on.

I remember an aunt who could not knit. She tried very hard, but no matter how hard she tried, she simply could not do it. She was a wonderful woman, and this frustrated her to the extent that she got very negative about it. However, when she discovered a knitting machine, there was no stopping her. Mechanics was something that she understood. Life throws all kinds of opportunities into your path, but that's not to say that all of those opportunities are ones at which you will excel. Accept that you can't do everything and start to celebrate the things that you can do.

There are several methods that you can use to get rid of self-doubt, and some of these have been covered in previous chapters. However, it's worth keeping a shortlist, so that you can easily refer to it and practice what it says:

☐ Switch off negative thoughts.

☐ Share positivity.

☐ Keep a journal of things for which you are grateful.

☐ Keep on looking within yourself for things you admire.

☐ Recognize what others say to you in the way of compliments.

☐ Learn from mistakes.

Make your own notes of several other things you can add to this list.

When you build molehills into mountains, you are making your own life difficult, and usually, this is done based upon sheer speculation. Instead of doing that, look at events in the past and work out the answers to "What would be the worst that could happen?" Then, work out the *best* thing that could happen, and work toward achieving it so that mistakes from the past become lessons for today, and you don't continue to make the same mistakes. When you do make mistakes, look at these as life lessons.

How many times have you heard your friends say things like "I am not falling for that again" or "I am not interested in men anymore"? What they are doing is getting past bad situations and trying to move on, but they are also learning from bad experiences so that in the future, they don't fall into the same trap. It's okay to tell yourself that you are moving forward and don't intend to be caught out again, but it's not alright to stop your life based upon your bad experiences. If you do this, you tend to hide from the world instead of embracing it and the opportunities it offers. Self-doubt can be an awful thing, but most of the time, if you do logical calculations on the events that made you feel like that, you will find there is no fault on your part. It was just circumstances. So, move the hurdle out of the way and move on. Looking backward will always trip you up.

Self-Doubt is Self-Defeating

When you approach a situation with an attitude that things will go wrong, they probably will –but not for the reasons you think. You may think that things go wrong because of your part in those events when that's only a small part of the picture. The hippo is coming out to haunt you again, and this time, he's remembering things you did in the past and using these against you. To stop this from happening, feed the hippo with positivity even when you are worried about something. Start telling yourself that you can get through this, rather than defeating yourself by feeding yourself negative feedback about your past failures. I will show you how to do this in the chapter relating to habits because when you treat the hippo to great food or positive thoughts, you really can tame it to respond to life more positively.

The negative fodder that you feed the hippo is being remembered. Every time you come across a new situation the hippo will be responsible for your negative responses. Thus, start to show your brain that you are in charge and that you are not prepared to fail without putting up a fight. Think hippo, and care for your hippo sufficiently to tell it that there are positive answers to everything that you currently perceive as being negative.

Let me give you an example of the hippocampus at work, to prove to you how it works. If you stay in a house where you get out of bed on the right-hand side every day, and then stay elsewhere where you have to get out on the left, you will find that for the first few days your mind is disorientated because your automatic response cannot happen and it makes you feel out of sorts. As soon as you go back to your own bed and you get used to getting out on the right-hand side, you confirm that habit and the hippocampus tell you that's what you need to do in the morning. However, what if you moved to a new house completely and forever? Or even if you moved your bed to a different position. For the first couple of weeks, the hippocampus needs to be educated to that new position of the bed, and the repetition of getting out on the other side becomes a habit. Until that habit is established, you will feel odd about getting out on the wrong side of the bed, but once he has learned that's the way it's going to be from now on, you won't have problems. The hippocampus can be reprogramed, and this simple example was to explain how it works and how it acts upon the things that you do in the course of your day by habit.

I can give you a funnier instance. Having recently moved to a new house, when I go to the toilet in the middle of the night, my hand reaches up to the right to get the toilet roll. For nearly 30 years, that's where it was. It's an automatic reaction. The hippocampus has not yet accepted that the toilet roll has moved, and it is only by habit that it will relearn this. Thus, if you feed yourself negative feedback and self-doubt, the hippocampus sees that as your normal response to life, and it will take a little while to make it think otherwise... but it can be done.

Reframing

When you spot self-doubt raising its ugly head, think straight away about reframing the problem so that you see it in a positive light. For example:

"I can't"

is replaced by

"I can learn how to do that ".

"I am no good at this"

is replaced by

"I am great at ...".

The whole point is that no one is good at everything, and if you go through life believing that you have to be, you are in for a disappointment. Just accept who you are without letting self-doubt creep into your mind. You have your strengths. There are things about you that are unique. Don't let self-doubt become one of them!

For example, I can't run a tidy home. It is not who I am, but I don't kick myself for it because there are other things I can do and excel at. Stop trying to be everyone's ideal and begin to be happy that you are your own ideal. That makes life a lot easier, and as you do this and approve of your actions instead of doubting them, your brain is learning more about the self-confident side of your character. In the habit section of this book are exercises that will help you to reinforce your strengths and get over any kind of self-doubt that you have. Remember that thoughts are nothing but thoughts, but repeated thoughts form habits. The kind of habits that you need to develop are positive ones, rather than negative ones, so don't keep repeating negative statements to yourself because they are self-defeating and will only lead to more self-doubt.

If someone was to ask me if I could stand on a stage and play the violin, I would laugh rather than feel incompetent. I can play the violin, but it's been years since I even touched one, and even then, it was a hobby my parents wished on me, rather than one I wanted to pursue. I am not afraid of saying "no" to those things outside my area of comfort. If someone wanted me to stand on my head for half an hour, I could possibly do that and would be willing to try, but the mistake that human beings make is doubting their abilities when in fact, their abilities may just be different from those demanded by others. You have strengths, and I want you to write them down and remember them. You have things that you are good at. Write them down and celebrate them, but just because you can't do everything, don't beat yourself up about it. We all have things that we cannot do, and that doesn't make us wrong. It simply means that we have other priorities.

Self-doubt should never stop you from trying something. If you don't want to do it, say so, and move on. If you don't think it's something you are that good at, say so and move on, but stop trying to impress everyone into liking you. I like loads of people who can't cook. I like many people who are not as practical as I am. The point is that your self-doubt makes you into less of a person than you have the right to be. Start to praise the things you can do and laugh at the mistakes that you make or learn from them. Self-doubt eats away at your confidence and makes you feel that you don't measure up, but why do you have to? The whole point is that none of us measure up to other people's standards and nor do we have to. We just have to measure up to our own standards. You will learn how to do that by changing habits, and those habits will go a long way toward taking away any self-doubts that you may have.

Habits are the framework of your life, which is why a chapter has been put aside to introduce you to habits that will change your life. If you doubt that you can adapt, then have no fear. These are habits that are simple to perform, and you won't be expected to step outside of your comfort level. What you don't know is that you have many habits already and it's simply a case of changing your habits and adopting new ones that help you to move forward without looking back at the moments of your life which have been spoiled by self-doubt. By the end of reading this book, you will not only believe in yourself, but you will have all of the self-esteem you need to be able to excel.

Chapter Five: Fears, Anxieties and Insecurities

"*Just when the caterpillar thought the world was ending, she became a butterfly.*" - Barbara Haines Howett

I want you to read the quotation above once more. The point is that there are times in your life when you read things wrong, and anxiety kicks in, when around the corner of chance lies the most wonderful discovery of all. You discover your capabilities, your dreams, your hopes, and your aspirations while anxiety is only a step away from that discovery. You just need help getting off this steppingstone and onto the next one.

Before we go further on this topic, you need to understand that all of the insecurities and anxieties that you feel come from inside your own head. That may sound a little harsh, but it's true. Yes, you may feel anxious about body image, but it's not the body image itself that is causing this. It's the way that you react to life in general after your emotions kick in to give their five cents' worth. Nothing that relates to anxiety and insecurity can do anything to your state of mind without the facilitation of emotions. Thus, if you control those emotions and know how they work, this helps you to build self-esteem and self-confidence. It's not how you look, but how your emotions carry you through certain situations that matter. Your mind may go into overdrive and feed you all kinds of negative statements that make sense to you at the time. Just like the caterpillar believed that it was the end of her life as she shed her coat, but discovered it was the beginning of something very beautiful, your anxieties are simply stepping stones to self-realization; learning to deal with them helps you to jump from one stepping stone to the next without becoming hurt in the process.

Your mind has set beliefs. Since you were a very small child, you have stored images in your mind concerning what you feel are acceptable pictures of who you should be. You have images such as:

☐ Someone who is confident

☐ Someone who is shy

☐ Someone who is motherly

☐ Someone who is cross or angry

☐ Someone who doesn't fit in

☐ Someone who is awkward and shy

Through the storybooks that you read as a child, you were introduced to all of these characteristics and know the difference between them, but it's very hard to visualize yourself when it comes to descriptions that are as intimate as this. The problem with these images is that somewhere along the line, you started to feel emotional because you didn't fit those images. That's what happens when self-esteem is low or when you don't have self-confidence. You may picture someone dressing in a certain way in your mind's eye or giving off certain body language based upon what your emotions know about it. The hippo has a huge memory. Perhaps you think of someone who is confident as a teacher that you had at school and measure yourself against that image. Perhaps you see the struggles of someone who is shy, and your personality avoids that trait. The point is that the whole of the human race has to come up against these differences every day; we see them in the people that we interact with and we start to set certain patterns that we feel are acceptable, and sometimes we find ourselves disappointed because we feel we don't measure up to our expectations of self.

The problem that you have created in your mind is that you are setting non-existent standards. In most areas of life, common sense will tell you how to behave and how not to behave, but apart from that, the rest is merely being guessed at by the whole world. You are not the only one with self-doubts, but instead of choking on them and making yourself wary of your stance on life, you should simply swallow them and not let them stop you from enjoying being you. Anxiety is a very wide spectrum within the realm of mental health, and, just like physical health, can affect the way that you interact with people and even the way you look at yourself. Think of the instance of someone who is physically ill. They don't have the patience to put up with visitors, and then feel anxious because they think they have been rude to people who care. The fact is that they are too ill to respond to normal conversation, and that's acceptable. Then look at it from a mental standpoint. If you are depressed, you may not want to talk to people, but then you kick yourself for being anti-social. Why? Is one of these illnesses less important than the other? Of course not. Anxiety can get so bad that you worry about everything, and turning that stress inward is not unusual for people who don't know how to express their thoughts outwardly.

So, what kind of behaviors would imply that you may have confidence or self-esteem problems when it comes to your day to day life? Insecurities and fears may be as follows:

☐ You may not feel that you measure up.

☐ You may worry that you haven't got what it takes.

☐ You may feel like you are a failure before you have even tried.

☐ You may not be able to face people in a confrontation.

☐ You may not be a good at arguing your point.

☐ You may allow others to walk all over you.

☐ You may not feel that you fit well into your perceived role in life.

☐ You may lack purpose.

The problem with all of these is that they can cause feelings of confusion. We have it thrown down our throats every day that we need to adhere to certain rules. Some take notice of what they see on their Facebook feed and see that as reality, while others may take their lead from the TV or the magazines that they read, but most of this insecurity comes from how comfortable you are in the skin you are in and the way that you have faced life up to this point. Bad experiences will contribute to negative self-image and anxiety. Let's examine the above points so you can see what's happening in each case.

Measuring Up

In this case, you may feel that your parents compared you with a sibling who was more successful than you or perhaps was their favorite. It's not a good start when you are compared because you go through life thinking that comparison is normal. However, no two individuals are the same, so the comparison is very unfair. If you were to look at the photos of girls of your age in magazines, some would be very pretty, while others may be fairly plain. Some will have amazing achievements in their lives, and some will have mediocre ones. The point about measuring up is that at some time in your life, you feel that you were compared, and if you carry on believing in comparisons, you will always measure your performance and be anxious about it. Instead of doing that, it's wise to understand where this came from in your thought patterns and then tell yourself that this is something you are going to stop in its tracks, using the habits detailed in the next chapter.

You Haven't Got What It Takes

This is too subjective to be true. It's a defeatist attitude, and it comes from negative thought processes and a lack of self-esteem, which both play on your emotional levels. It's not realistic, and when you are in a better frame of mind, you will find that you do indeed have what it takes and that this frame of mind is simply caused by being overwhelmed. When you learn to control that, as you will from the habits included in the next chapter, you need never be overwhelmed again. It's very much in the same category as feeling you are a failure before you even try something.

All of these defeatist attitudes are happening for a reason, and it's not the reason you may think it is. It has nothing to do with the thoughts being true. It has everything to do with anxiety and how it makes you feel. If you accept that your anxiety is fueling more anxiety and insecurity, then you can start to work toward making yourself feel more capable and deserving.

Fears are born through experience as well as expectations. We live in a period when instant gratification is pushed as the norm but is it really as viable as you think? For instance, fear comes from many areas in a woman's life, including the following:

☐ Fear of loneliness

☐ Fear of poverty

☐ Fear of pregnancy

☐ Fear of childlessness

☐ Fear of getting old

☐ Fear of our weight being out of control

We place far too many expectations on our own shoulders because of what we perceive as social norms. Fear stokes the fires of insecurity, and thus these are areas that a woman needs to be aware of so that she can protect herself from emotional harm. The strong and confident woman has none of these fears because she has learned to take life at a pace that suits her and her lifestyle. This chapter is merely intended to outline how differently women perceive things when compared to men. Men are the providers and will fight tooth and nail to provide. Women, on the other hand, are more complex, and without even being aware of it, they will think of life from the perspective of their emotional state. A woman's hormonal differences to her male counterpart are obvious, and the biggest difference will be seen in the testosterone levels, which is normally higher in men and lower in their female counterparts.

When you consider the number of people who suffer from anxiety disorders, the numbers are frightening. Women suffer more than men; statistics show that the figure for women is 23 percent higher than that of men. That isn't meant to belittle the stress experienced by men at all but is only shown to emphasize that it's quite probable that a woman will suffer from anxiety or stress at some time in their lives, particularly between the puberty and the age of 50. The symptoms of an anxiety disorder can include:

- ☐ Breathing difficulties
- ☐ Higher blood pressure
- ☐ Increased heart rate
- ☐ Panic attacks
- ☐ Finding difficult to concentrate for extended periods
- ☐ Experiencing gastric problems
- ☐ Finding it difficult to sleep

It all sounds pretty scary, but many of these symptoms are a byproduct of other symptoms. For example, the increased heart rate will come about because of higher blood pressure, and panic attacks may be precipitated by difficulty in sleeping or being unable to breathe correctly. The difficulty in concentration may simply be because you didn't get sufficient rest; the gastric problems may stem from the fact that because of your nervousness, you ate too quickly or didn't chew the food correctly. The point of this chapter is to let you know what's going on inside and why it causes fears, anxiety, and insecurities. The whole-body package counts, rather than one symptom simply being thought of as a unique symptom not affecting other parts of your body or its functions. The body is in harmony when you are happy and healthy, and that's important to note, especially if you suffer from one or two symptoms at a time.

Insecurities, on the other hand, are usually caused by a lack of confidence. Perhaps this has come about because you have had experiences in the past where you felt that you have failed. The hippocampus has remembered that feeling of failure and keeps reminding you of it when you attempt to do anything of a similar nature. This is where the re-education of the hippocampus becomes a necessary part of growth.

The next chapter is extensive, so you need a choose a time to read it when you can take in what's being said and use the exercises included in the chapter to try to work out solutions to your insecurities and your anxieties. When you take the actions suggested in that chapter, you will see improvements that may surprise you. It's a case of understanding what you are doing to yourself through your thought processes and then turning them around so that you no longer feel anxious about your place in the world. You are a human being with normal feelings and emotions, but you just haven't learned to use them for your betterment, rather than to make you feel less than complete. Once you do, you will find that life gets better, and you gain self-esteem and begin to like the person that you have become. So will the hippo! He doesn't like working hard on negative things, and if you can make him happy, you make yourself happy at the same time.

You have the power to remove the anxiety from your life, and when you develop the habits that are outlined in the next chapter, expect success, because each one of the habits listed has been proven to work. You will even find that Oprah Winfrey and other celebrities perform similar habits, and their lives are a testament to the efficiency of the habits you are about to introduce into your life.

Chapter Six: 8 Habits that Boost Self-Esteem

"I have learned that champions are not just born. Champions can be made when they embrace and commit to life-changing positive habits."
– Lewis Howes

    Self-esteem can be boosted by taking certain actions, and this chapter is all about those boosts to your self-esteem. These take place little by little and become habitual ways of facing every new day. Habits are formed easily, although initially, you will need to work out what habits are beneficial, and this chapter will help you to embrace habits that help in self-development rather than those that shrink the importance of who you are. When you take on a new habit, try to make it something that you do daily, so that it becomes who you are rather than something you have to work at in the future. When you perform habits each day, then the hippocampus remembers these responses, and it won't be long before you are performing those habits without having to prompt yourself. I want you to watch a video made by Oprah Winfrey on the subject of Believing in Yourself. You can make such a difference in your life by changing your habits. Remember, if you repeat an action over and over again, it makes your hippocampus remember your reaction and repeat it in the future.

Thus, although it may take a little bit of effort at first, when the hippocampus knows this is your priority, you will be doing all of these things on autopilot, requiring very little effort on your part. That's why these habits work and are the secret to self-esteem and happiness.

Habit Number One – Dress for Self-Confidence

There's nothing quite as frustrating as finding that the dress you saw on someone stunning doesn't suit you or do your figure any favors. It makes you feel inferior to that person in some way, but the fact is that different women have different body shapes, and it's important to get to know yours. There will be certain outfits that make you feel good about yourself, while others do nothing to boost your self-esteem. You may have trouble imagining something called "enclothed cognition," but when I explain what this means, you will get a better idea about it. When scientists wanted to find out if clothing made any difference to the self-image, they found something pretty startling. At Northwestern University, an experiment on clothing was done by introducing people to different kinds of clothing to see whether their level of concentration was affected by the clothing that they were asked to wear. The typical response by those who were asked to wear a white doctor's jacket was much more pronounced than when being asked to wear a painter's outfit. We assume that there are intelligence levels attached to different jobs and therefore perceive the doctor's job as requiring more intelligence than the painter's job. It may not be so, but it is what our perceptions tell us.

We also dress in a certain manner for different occasions. For example, when you wear your casual clothing, you are not expecting to be placed in a formal situation. Thus, wearing your jeans and sweater at home is quite normal. However, dressing is more than all of this, and the more comfortable you feel in the clothing you wear, for the situation that you have to face, the better. A smart suit for an interview is normal apparel by society norms, though some people don't seem to get that it's not just about the suit. It's about how comfortable the person in the suit is, and that starts with the underwear that you wear. If you wear a bra that is two sizes too small, simply because you don't want to admit you have put on weight, for example, you actually emphasize the lumps and bumps. Therefore, when you put on your outer garments, those bumps and lumps are visible. However, if you buy the correct size (and take the labels off if you don't want anyone to know what size you take) you smooth the lines of your clothing.

A 2014 survey of women asked what women felt made them feel the most confident, and in their answers, they included the classic black dress, high heels, and a great perfume. However, you can feel confident in colors that suit your personality as well as styles that make you feel good about the way that you look. The added perfume is simply your way of saying, "I feel good about me."

The psychology of the way that you dress says a lot about who you are and what you feel about yourself. For example, someone who perpetually hides their figure behind baggy clothing isn't making the most of themselves but is, in fact, drawing attention to themselves. There are also body parts that will dictate what's best to wear and a woman who knows what her strong points are will dress so that those strong points are what people see. Scarves and accessories are a great way to make a dull outfit shine, and colors introduced into your wardrobe should be those that suit your skin shade and that enhance your hair color. The overall look is the thing that you are trying to create, and when you get it right, you will psychologically know that you have and feel that you can face the world without inner turmoil about your clothing or the way people look at you.

Habit Number Two: Take It to The Tribe

For a moment, think about friends that you know and trust. These are usually people who make you feel good about being who you are. The fact that you can choose your friendships is a bonus that many do not take. For example, if someone makes you feel small, why do you spend so much time being influenced by that negativity? For the sake of this exercise, write down a list of people that you know and divide them into three columns. The first column will be casual friendships, or perhaps people you know from work but don't have any real contact with them outside of the workplace. Then you have the column of people you cannot avoid. These may be family and friends of the family with whom you are not close, but who will nonetheless influence the way you feel about yourself.

The last column is the tribe. These are people you tell your secrets to. They are the folks who stand by you through thick and thin and who don't mind listening to your woes as well as sharing your victories. These are the most important influences on your self-esteem, as they make you feel good about yourself. The idea of this exercise is to weigh how much time you spend with each type of person. The second group can include people you know through your family but who are emotionally draining or friends that you once trusted but who use you. One of the least healthy types of friendship is the user, as this is a person who will make you feel that you are there to listen to them but who never listen to you. They are the people who ask favors but never return them. These are one-sided relationships that are almost toxic to your self-esteem and who make you feel like someone else's doormat.

It's vital to divide your time more beneficially so that you spend more time with your true tribe – those who love and understand you and who like you as you are. These are people who will build self-esteem and make you feel good about who you are. If you can divide your time a little more efficiently so that you get to hang out with those people more, then you will certainly increase your self-esteem. People who use you are breaking your self-esteem down, so you need to learn to say "no," even if you feel that you don't have a valid excuse. Excuses are not necessary, and although the first time is always the hardest, they will soon get the message and move on to someone else who is willing to do their bidding. The power that you gain from making your own choices will have been worth it.

Habit Number Three: Asserting Who You Are

Sometimes it is hard to say what you want to say because people with a lack of self-esteem don't feel that they can stick up for themselves when it comes to even small things like saying "No", but the fact is that you empower others when you keep saying "yes" all the time and don't have it in you to say "no." Why give away that right? There is a very good way that you can help yourself to get over this hump. If you have something more important to do, then you won't feel as bad about asserting your views to others. For example, if you do voluntary work at the local dog shelter or help out with something locally that takes up some of your time, you not only get to feel better about yourself, but you also find that you have less time in which to say "yes" to people who don't deserve your help. These are, as explained above, people who use you or take you for granted. Once in a while, it empowers you to be able to say "no, sorry, I am busy", and to simply make them sort their own problems out. Another way in which you can assert yourself is by being influenced by your real friends about what makes you look good and stop giving in to those relatives who insist on buying you awful clothing items.

Denise was very influenced by her parents and found that she couldn't make her own choices because they were always making choices for her. Then she discovered how to assert herself without offending anyone simply by telling them that she preferred to do something else, or that she preferred to wear something else. You see, though our parents are there to guide us through the initial phases of our lives, they are not our keepers. They know that eventually you will grow up and make your own decisions. When Denise understood what assertiveness could do for her self-esteem, she made changes, and they were life changing. In fact, she was quite shocked at the respect that she gained from her parents for being able to make her own decisions instead of relying so heavily upon them.

What Are You Doing When You Assert Yourself?

You are expressing opinions, and every person on earth is entitled to have an opinion. If you decide who you are going to vote for, it's recognized as your right, but it's also self-assertive. No one else knows whose name you put a cross next to, so in effect, you are making up your own mind. You may be influenced by others and have been brought up to believe certain things, but if you make your mind up as to which candidate is best because you understand what they stand for, and choose them, then this is self-assertion. Under the law, you are not answerable to anyone as to whom you chose to vote for. However, take it outside of the polling booth, and you start to worry about offending people, or you start to worry about whether you've got what it takes to make decisions. Some people grow up and get married still lacking assertion skills, and will let their partners make all of the decisions, but that's never a good way to go because self-assertion says, "Hey, there's two people in this relationship and both of us count." It makes you count for something. It doesn't mean being contrary for the sake of it. What it does mean is that if you have a point of view, you are entitled to express it.

What you are doing to yourself is pretty amazing. You are reinforcing who you are, and thus it's a little like affirmations. Each time you decide on your own, you are reinforcing the fact that you are capable of making decisions. You may make mistakes from time to time, but that's human too, and if you learn to laugh at those mistakes

-if they aren't too grave- or learn from them for the future -if they are important- then your assertion isn't wasted. However, never think that self-assertion is rudeness or that it's something you are not entitled to. You do it every day without even knowing it. Let's show you some examples:

☐ I must get out of bed

☐ I am going to wear a red dress today

☐ I am going to have eggs for breakfast

☐ I am going to walk to work today because it's sunny

Every action you take in your day is an assertion in one way or another, and self-assertion is the difference between someone making you get out of bed, someone insisting that you wear the blue dress when you planned to wear the red one, someone making you have toast instead of eggs for breakfast, or someone insisting that you drive to work on that sunny day. Do you see how it works? You put yourself into the driving seat of your life by making assertions, and each time you do, you build a little more solid foundation for who you are and who you will become. Each time you let others assert things that rule your life, you give them the power instead and start to shrink back from life - almost like living in the shadows.

Step out of the shadows of your life and start making decisions about what's going to happen today, and you start to feel like a whole human being instead of having your life dictated to you by other people. Of course, in the work environment, you have to do what your boss tells you, but imagine that feeling of being able to explain to your boss a quicker way of doing mundane tasks, or being able to show your boss that you know more than he gives you credit for. These all help you in the bid to assert who you are. Similarly, in an interview for a job, change your mindset. Ask yourself how much you want the job and how valuable you know that you are. Often when you are selling yourself in a situation like this, it pays to be convinced that you have a lot to offer, rather than to shrink into a corner not knowing what to say. Be bold in your life and learn that assertion is merely about expressing an opinion, and you won't go far wrong.

Look at the cases above, where it becomes apparent that you were able to make up your mind about things like getting out of bed, etc. Now, look at other choices in the same way. If you go to dinner with friends and you don't want to eat French fries, tell them you are on a restricted diet. It's not inconvenient, and you are entitled to assert yourself. If someone offers you coffee and you prefer tea, then say so. A little bit of assertion every day will help you to become more confident and improve your self-esteem, but they don't have to be major things. As you go through this exercise, write down what you achieved in each day for the next seven days by speaking your mind instead of just making do. You have a voice, and now is the time to start to exercise it.

Habit Number Four: Using Affirmations

I know you have probably laughed about the idea of telling yourself you are beautiful every time that you look in the mirror, or that this will make you beautiful. However, if you look seriously into the subject of affirmations and also understand about how the brain works, it's easy to see a pattern. Feed your mind negative statements, and all that you attract into your life is negativity. You feel bad about being you. You lose confidence and lack self-esteem, and all of this negative feedback is adding to the bleakness of your life. It follows quite logically that if you can reframe the things that you say to yourself into positive statements – or affirmations – then the opposite happens. Let's look at some of the things you are likely to say to yourself regularly:

- ☐ I can't do this
- ☐ I can't wear something like that
- ☐ I look fat

- [ ] I won't get the job
- [ ] I am out of my league

The problem here is that the longer you repeat this to the hippocampus, the more it believes it, and you are powering up the negativity so that your own negativity hits your confidence levels. However, if you reframe everything and look at every aspect of your life as an opportunity rather than a dread, you will find yourself capable of doing much more than you originally gave yourself credit for. Let's look at some positive affirmations that may help you to start your day in the right way.

- [ ] The sun is shining, and I am starting my day off with optimism
- [ ] Even the clouds have a silver lining, and thing will get better today
- [ ] I love getting up early and enjoying a relaxing breakfast
- [ ] I love taking care of myself and enjoying my walking hours

All of these are positive statements that give you a little bit of a buzz to start your day. Energy is at its highest in the morning, but if you start the day with negativity, the level of negativity is also high, and that will hold you back from enjoying your life. The kind of affirmations that work is not the "I could...." Affirmations, because the "I am" affirmations are more powerful. Let me give you a demonstration of someone who believed that he would win the lottery. He was so convinced that he would win that he started to think positively, similarly to someone who already had the money. His logic was not flawed. If you want to be rich, you can't think like a poor man. His affirmations included things like:

- [ ] I know how to manage my money
- [ ] I know how to attract money toward me

These are just money-oriented, and in your case, we want to create realistic affirmations that use all of your positive attributes to give you more confidence. They must have a certain element of truth, and you need to change your approach each day toward thinking of all the nice things about yourself, rather than dwelling on what you see as weak points. There is absolutely nothing wrong with celebrating who you are or even feeling smug sometimes about the little things that you achieve. Start giving yourself more goals that you can achieve and then use affirmations to congratulate yourself, and soon you will find that affirmations come naturally to you. For instance, you always leave the kitchen a mess in the morning. Change tack. Put away the dishes and then tell yourself, "I am tidy and clean and can organize my life." Then when you have a habit of being late to meetings, turn up early. Tell yourself, "I am always prepared for the things I need to do." Although you may take a little convincing at the start, if you get into the habit of doing this with all of the tasks you do each day, you drown out the negative voice and fill your mind with positivity about who you are and what you represent. Affirmations can be used in all areas of your life. For example, whenever you feel positive about something, note it mentally and tell yourself you are good at that thing, because the affirmations you make from these feel-good moments are worth it and you are basing them on actual fact, so you can't question whether they are true or not. Affirmations are not about intentions. They are about who you are and what you are and should always be positive and reinforcing so that you see improvements in your ability to mix with different kinds of people as well as noting an improvement in the way that you view yourself.

- ☐ I am great with kids and love animals
- ☐ I have a heart filled with love for others
- ☐ I am thoughtful and kind
- ☐ I am a person who succeeds
- ☐ My friends like me

Of course, there are many more that you can add to it. After cooking a successful meal, you may want to add "I am a great cook," and this may help you to have less doubt when you have to cook for the company. All of these things are positive notions that you repeat to yourself so that they become your way of thinking. Think success; be successful. It works because your hippocampus will eventually pull out all of these affirmations and see them as being something worth holding onto so that you can approach new situations from a more positive perspective.

Habit Number Five: Adopt a Goddess Mindset

You may be asking yourself what kind of nonsense this is but bear me out because you must listen to me. The Goddess Mindset is something that is inherently a part of being a woman. As you grow up, it's there waiting for you to take advantage of it, and during your teens, you probably have seen it from time to time, when you look in the mirror and feel really good about who you are. Little by little, life tends to chip away at it and make you question your values. That's when the Goddess Mindset gets crushed, and women become less than they ever intended to be. In fact, they lose themselves in the process.

Let's take this back to basics. Do you remember when you were a little girl and perhaps thought of yourself as a princess? No? Well, as far back as that, that little Goddess inside you was telling you who you were, and you instantly became that person. The princess was just a small part of it. The girl who made a wonderful cake at school may have thought of herself as the next trend in cooking, or the girl who sang could imagine herself as the next Madonna. However, the Goddess mindset develops or disintegrates, depending upon your image of who you are. The first line of questioning to ascertain whether you have the Goddess Mindset is:

- ☐ Do you trust yourself?
- ☐ Do you believe in yourself?
- ☐ Are you the best person you think you can be?

If you have any doubts about any of these questions, then you need to work on gaining that knowledge of yourself that allows you to answer them in the affirmative. The trust issue is easy. If you promise something, do you follow through? If you say you will help a friend, do you do it? Issues such as false promises may come from things such as wanting to slim or wanting to give up cigarettes, but these are temporary situations rather than core values. Core values that make up the inner Goddess mindset are those that say that you know who you are and like who you are. You believe in yourself, and you see yourself at your best at this moment in time. It's not about the fancy dress you wear. It's about how you feel in the skin you are in. Some wonderful videos on YouTube cover this subject, and from people you may not identify as Goddesses. They may not be the most beautiful women. They may not be all style and show, but the one thing that these women have in common is that they truly believe they are the best that they can be and will go on improving on that so that they remain that way rather than getting complacent in their approach to life.

There are two methods of getting your Goddess Mindset. One is to remind yourself of all the nice things that you do in life and to build upon this foundation, and the other is distinctly different; instead of thinking outside of your own needs, to the needs of others, you need to stop making comparisons of yourself with other people's expectations of you. When push comes to shove, all that matters is that you spend time with people YOU approve of, rather than seeking approval from others or taking notice of what other people think about you. Their thoughts are of small significance to your life unless you let them become significant, and that's where the Goddess mindset comes into play. I am who I am, but can other people around me measure up? It's a case of reverse psychology. For example, when you go out on a date, stop worrying about how you will appear to the person you are dating. Start to concentrate your attention on questions such as "Will he live up to expectations? Will he amuse me? Will he be funny and quirky?" You are not judging. What you are doing is taking the focus away from who you are and working out if people fit into your life. If they don't, then they have no right to be there.

I have mentioned hanging out with your crowd or your tribe, but it doesn't just mean those people who make you happy. It also means those people who will, of course, give you the job, those people who will be positive in their approach, and certainly those people who recognize you for the goddess that you are.

Let the goddess come out to play sometimes. Be that Princess, be that special someone because when you stop letting yourself enjoy the liberation of just being you, you start to measure yourself, and that helps no one. You start to worry about what you have to give instead of being rightly worried about who you want in your life and who will help you to retain that goddess. If someone stifles your creativity, for example, should you live with it? Or should you make a point of allowing your creativity to come out in another way? You have to cater to the goddess, or you will lose her, and many women give up the right to be a goddess when they stop pleasing themselves and start to depend upon pleasing others.

Habit Number Six: Meditation

A lot of women that I work with don't really know the meaning of meditation and don't like the idea because it's beyond the scope of their knowledge. However, when they introduce it and practice it daily, I have them running to me with stories about how free they feel and how capable of expressing themselves they have become. Their confidence soars. Their ability to mix with people is extraordinary, and their acceptance of self is undeniable. You may not know it, but that part of the woman's brain that deals with emotions needs to be left to its own devices sometimes. The rush of thoughts and the amount of multi-tasking that we subject it to isn't what it was designed for.

I told you before about the hippocampus – our friend who registers our important actions and memories. The hippocampus changes new habits and incorporates them into the day-to-day activities that you do, so it's a very good thing to feed the hippo with all of the right kinds of food. Let me show you what happens when you meditate:

Your blood pressure goes down – That's going to stop you from having panic attacks and will enable you to be more in control of your life.

Your heart rate slows – This is going to benefit heart health and longevity.

Your mind is emptied of clutter – This is a wonderful side effect of meditation because it helps you to have a clear mind and see things for what they really are without blowing everything up into a panic. If you lack confidence, you will gain it through meditation because you are no longer stuffing your mind full of negativity.

You will learn not to judge people or situations – Have you ever had a conversation with someone, thought about what they said, and then exaggerated it so much that you have all kinds of ideas about the conversation that make it a mental burden to you? People, especially those who lack self-esteem, read things into what others say. They ask themselves things like:

☐ Does he really like me, or is he just being polite?

☐ Is she trying to make me look good with that dress or trying to make a fool of me?

☐ Does that color really suit me, or were people just being polite?

☐ Does this hairstyle really look good, or are people just being kind?

These are thoughts that would be classed by people who meditate as being the "monkey mind." It's the part of you that has conversations with itself and who makes mountains out of molehills. Well, meditation quietens down that part of the mind so that you are not afraid of silence, not afraid of being alone, and certainly not afraid of letting nature help you to heal. Meditation declutters all of the boxes of thoughts that you have been tossing around in your head and seals those boxes so that you can think only about *now*, and quite frankly, that's the only time that really matters. If you made a mistake in the past, you can't undo it. You can apologize if you think you hurt someone, but you can't change what you did. It's over, and it's done with, and with meditation, you learn to catch up with yourself and be here and now, rather than in the land of regrets and remorse. Both of those words are negative and will not help confidence at all. Mistakes are mistakes, and the only way to get past them is to learn from them; meditation clears your mind sufficiently to do that.

So, What's Special About Meditation?

It means sitting in a quiet place in a certain pose so that energy can run through you as you breathe. You concentrate on the breathing method that is given to you for a purpose. It's not to avoid thoughts. It is simply to show you that you can think of things that are more productive and not prioritize your emotional problems and dramas. It helps you to let your body heal you, rather than trying to do this with your conscious thoughts. The one benefit that I have found from meditation -which is why I teach women to do this daily- is that you feel refreshed and at peace with the world, instead of always being at odds with it. You are more creative, and you also learn what's happening inside your body when you breathe, and have a lot more respect for your body. It makes you feel at one with the world, and when that happens, you can use it during your day for short moments, simply to remind yourself of what YOU are all about, rather than letting the world around you twist who you are into someone with self-esteem issues and lack of confidence. All of the negative thoughts that you have come from inside your head and meditation helps you to put those aside and to realize that your true potential lies in knowing yourself and loving who you are.

So, What Does Happen in the Body When You Meditate?

You have something inside you called the sympathetic nervous system. This does many jobs within the body, such as controlling temperatures or making sure that the right amount of oxygen is pumped to all the right places. When you breathe in the way that you are taught for meditation, you help to regulate what's happening in your body. You awaken your intuition, that little voice that tells you what's good for you and what's not, the one that you may not have been listening to for a while. Altogether, the sympathetic nervous system is put into overdrive and works more efficiently so that you feel better, but you also need to feed yourself with good nourishing food and make sure that you drink sufficient water and get enough sleep. All of these body issues get in the way of your happiness if they are neglected. Meditation pulls you back into the positive loop so that you know which direction your life is going in and are happier with who you are and what life offers you.

Many of the physical symptoms that women feel throughout their lives are dictated by the release of hormones within the body. Your monthly venture into womanhood is part of this process, but some women go through an awful time while others sail through. Meditation helps you to balance pain and helps the brain to know which hormones to release to make you feel good about life. That solid foundation for your life is brought about by a twenty-minute-a-day habit of meditating, so it's not a huge price to pay. It is such an enormous subject that I have decided to devote the next part of this chapter to it to do it justice. I do hope that you will enjoy what you read and will be able to use it in your life.

How to Meditate

The first thing that you need to decide is where you can meditate. It should be a place where you will not be disturbed and where you feel comfortable; if you set up an area in which to meditate, it tends to enthuse you, and you are investing yourself into the habit. You may need a yoga mat and a supportive cushion, but if you have limited mobility you can use a specific chair, which should be a hard chair with a straight back. However, you can make the whole experience of meditation a little more motivating by adding things that you find inspirational around your chosen area, such as candles or a Buddha statue or a few favorite plants. When you meditate, you are not worshipping at all, so it has no bearing on what religion you follow. You simply use the Buddha statue or whatever you choose for inspiration. It could even be a photo of someone dear to you or a vase of flowers.

The seating position for meditation, if you use a cushion, is to sit with your back straight and then bend the knees and cross the ankles. Make sure that you are centered by swaying right and left until you are sure you are comfortable. Then place your hands on your lap with the palms facing upward and one hand cupping the other. Touch your thumbs together. If you are using a chair, sit with your back straight, and do not be tempted to lean back. Place your feet flat on the floor. You can also place your hands on your lap, as in the cushion position.

Make sure that you have comfortable clothes that are not going to distract you by chafing or binding. That's very important because there's nothing like a tight waistband to take your mind off meditation. Now, start to breathe, in through the nostrils to the count of 8, and then out to the count of 10. It's not like your normal breathing, which is relatively shallow. In the case of meditation, it's purposeful breathing, and the idea is that you sink into this moment in the breath, and that means concentrating solely on what's happening to your body as you breathe, rather than letting external thoughts get into the way.

You need to continue to do this until you feel that the pattern of breathing is taking on a rhythm. Then, continuing to breathe in and breathe out, at the end of each cycle of inhalation and exhalation, you count one, then two, then three, etc.

The idea of meditation is clearing the mind, so if you get any thoughts that come to your mind while you are meditating, you simply let them go. Do not judge them, and do not let them form a chain of thoughts in your mind. Just let them go. They may be things that you need to deal with at a later time, but now is not the time to think about them. Let go and breathe. If you need to concentrate on anything, think about the air going down into your body and the way it leaves the body, and be aware of movements within your body that happen while you are breathing. You are in this moment, and traveling in your mind to other moments is what you are trying not to do. In fact, you are not really even trying. You are simply letting go and letting yourself be at this moment in time. Keep this up for around 20 minutes each morning when you get up and over the next week or so, you will begin to notice a difference in your approach to life. Don't expect sudden changes as there won't be any. Just go with the flow, and if thoughts come to your head, don't kick yourself for them. It's a natural progression, and learning to let go is the hardest part, but it doesn't require concentration. When you concentrate on something, you take away the spontaneity of it, so just go with the flow and allow yourself to breathe and count, breathe and count. Remember what I said about your blood pressure and heart rate? These will go down during meditation, so you must not get up quickly when you think that you have finished. Instead of doing this, it's a good idea to have a journal next to you so that you can record what you felt at the end of a meditation session and make notes on how you think you can improve that meditation the next time around. Perhaps some things distracted you during the meditation, and you can move them for next time so that you don't experience that same irritation again.

There are other ways to meditate that may be helpful to you. If you feel that your eyes need something to look at while you meditate, then guided meditation is a good way to go. In this case, you will choose something to concentrate your eyes on while you breathe, and this can be the flame of a candle or a statue or even a photograph of someone who inspires you. However, if you have never meditated before, I suggest that meditation with the eyes closed is a lot easier because you take away the potential of distraction. Meditation doesn't work magic that you can notice straight away. It clears the mind so that you can make better decisions. It makes the liaison between the mind and body more pronounced so that you care more about your place in the world and take action to make yourself healthier and happier. It's a great foundation upon which to build yourself because you let go of all of the things that do not form parts of that moment, such as past hurts or future worries.

You may not know it, but you can use meditation anywhere. Simply close your eyes and breathe and be oblivious to what's happening around you. It's useful before a stressful meeting or when you are going for an interview. It helps to sharpen your mind and can be used to calm down the stresses and strains that life imposes upon you. Are you meeting someone new for the first time? Breathe in and out as you do with meditation before meeting them, and you are likely to be less nervous. Worried about taking some exams? Breathe in and out and close your eyes for a moment before entering the exam room. You have the necessary skills to pass those exams. What detracts from them is the nervousness that your mind imposes on yourself, and meditation helps to set the balance right. Meditation helps you in so many areas of your life, and once you learn to take it with you through your life, you take that sense of calm with you and let go of your anxieties forever. Being this aware of your state of mind helps you to be stronger so that anxieties have the opposite effect on you and simply make you more convinced that there are always solutions.

Habit Number Seven: Do What You Love ANYWAY

Each day when you get out of bed, you surround yourself with familiarity. You get used to doing certain things and having certain habits, but what if I told you that it's okay to let go and let the inner child out sometimes? You would probably laugh it off and not even attempt it, but it is worth it, and soon you will know why. People hold themselves back because they believe that society expects them to behave in a certain way, and yes, to a degree, politeness is expected, and being decent to others is common sense, but what about the rest of it? Are you typecast? If you are overweight, for example, would you avoid going to the gym? If you are skinny, would you avoid the beach because you feel you will be criticized? Often people with self-esteem issues make those issues larger than life by giving up on things that they love doing, but that they feel self-conscious about doing. Ellen loved to act but was always typecast into roles that were minor because the mistress at her school did not believe her body fit the roles that Ellen wanted. We let ourselves down when we stop doing something we love simply because society expects us to take a back seat.

To do what you love to do, you have to know what it is that you perceive as being something you really would love to do. It's no good saying that life won't let you do things and being vague about it, so you need to take the following steps, so you can do the things you love:

Step One: Know What You Want to Do

There's nothing wrong with writing into a journal the things that you want to do in your life. No one is going to live your life for you, and if you love doing these things, no one has the right to stop you. For example, Sara wanted to make patchwork quilts, but she never really gave herself the time to do it. She got around this by allowing herself a small amount of time each day to quilt and gradually got more proficient, ending up several years later giving demonstrations of quilting and even having her own exhibition. If you can't pinpoint the things that you want to do, you will never achieve them, so work out your bucket list of things you want to do, even if these are tiny things that bring you joy and laughter. Helen wanted to jump in a puddle. She had lived in the city most of her life and had seen kids doing this in the country and had this vision of joy in her mind about doing it and not caring about getting wet. She waited, but she kept it on her bucket list and actually did it, and that feeling gave her new confidence that all of her goals, no matter how big or small, were possibilities rather than simply dreams.

Step Two: Find Out What Obstacles are Getting in Your Way

For this step, you need to look realistically at what's stopping you from doing those things that you see yourself doing to give yourself joy. If it's money, you can save and work toward accruing a nest egg. If it's a case of feeling you don't have a voice, give yourself one. If you feel that life is not giving you time, make that time. You have to work out what's stopping you and then work on taking away those obstacles because you are the only one who can.

Step Three: Live the Life You Imagined and Start Today

We can all close our eyes and imagine what will bring joy into our lives, but if you find things that truly make you feel good, then you need to start to make those things happen. Don't let others stop you. Don't let your shyness or your self-esteem issues get in the way because it's only you who sees those negative thoughts, and others around you are struggling just as much as you are to get their voices heard. Yet, every day we read stories of women who have started doing what they love and making their lives fulfilled and enjoyable. You can, too. You need to create the ideal picture of who you are rather than worry about how you are perceived. Be the best person that you can be to fit in with the joys you want to encompass in your life.

Habit Number Eight: Share your Story

How many women do you imagine feeling the way that you do? Perhaps there are millions, because looking at the state of mental health all over the world, we know that the numbers of illnesses that are related to self-esteem and self-doubt are on the rise. One of the most inspirational websites I ever read was a blog written by a woman who suffered from self-esteem issues. She wasn't afraid to tell her story, and the inspiration that it gave to many women all over the world was amazing. She started out very unsure of herself, but as her story unfolded, so did the comments from other women who had suffered similar self-esteem issues who no longer felt that they were alone and who were able to build each other up through mutual support by showing total honesty about their fears in life and what they had done to overcome them.

Although you may not feel like a leader at this stage, the feedback that you get from blogs is very sensitive; people like you don't get slammed for being who they are. Women all over the world are looking for solutions to their problems. They are not looking for problems, and the comment section on each page of your personal blog can be inspirational and help you to see that you do not lack in any way at all. Being able to express yourself in words is helpful from a therapeutic point of view as well, and many women have used this platform to make others aware of what it feels like to be lacking in confidence and self-esteem. Did you know that writing your life story can be liberating? It helps with freeing all of those negative thoughts so that you don't have to relive them every day. You are letting them out onto the page, and psychologically this can be extremely powerful in the search for self-esteem.

If you decide to go this route, then make sure that you have a good audience, by learning all about keywords because it is these words that lead people to your blog. Many blog sites have helpful forums to tell you how to draw attention to your blog and place it in the right category so that the right people see it. You can also link it to a Facebook account and find many readers through your social networking sites.

If you are a little wary of letting friends and family know about how you feel, then create a Facebook account just for this purpose and befriend others who may be interested in reading a woman's story; you will be surprised how many are. It's a boost to your self-esteem, and if you keep your stories up to date and interesting, you really can help others by helping yourself.

The habits that have been included in this section are all healthy habits that you can make into a part of your everyday life. When you embrace these habits, you will find that you are more creative, happier, more well-accepted and that your self-esteem will be boosted by the results that you get. I have seen so many women turn their lives around simply by adopting these habits and making themselves surer of their footing in the world. The work that you put into learning these habits will make a true difference to the way that people react toward you and increase your acceptance of the fact that everyone has different choices that are right for them. Just because yours seem a little different doesn't make them wrong. It merely means that you are exercising your individuality, and that's going to help you to like who you are and accept yourself.

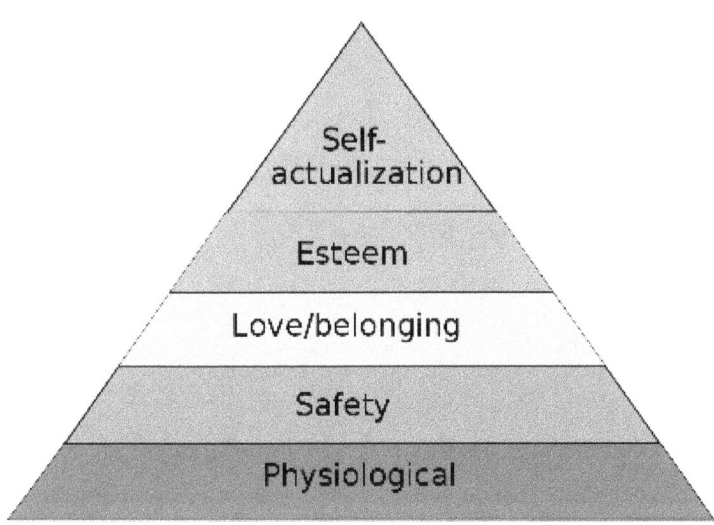

Self-esteem is a great asset to have on your side. It means self-acceptance, and it also means recognizing when you shine and when your halo needs a little more polish. You are a wonderful human being but have let life cut you down to size. Now it's time to fight back and show the world that your stature is complete and that you are happy to be in your own skin. When you do, the law of attraction will work in your favor. I am not sure if you are familiar with the law of attraction, but positive people are magnets for other positive people, while misery only encourages abusive relationships and unhappy people. When you learn what your talents are, celebrate them. Make small goals for yourself and celebrate your successes. Your thoughts dictate to a very large extent how you perceive yourself and your daily meditation will help to keep those in check.

Chapter Seven: Why Self-Care is Important

"Follow your heart, listen to your inner voice, stop caring about what others think."   -Roy T. Bennett

A long time ago, a psychologist named Maslow made a chart of all of the things that you need in your life in order to feel happy. It was a very clever chart made in the '40s but is still relevant today. I am going to show you the different levels of that chart and explain to you why each of them is relevant to happiness and self-fulfillment.

The elements that make up this chart are fairly obvious ones, but it may not be as obvious why these needs are important. The first line is physiological needs. That's the food that you eat and the water that you drink, as well as the shelter you need and the feeling of wellbeing that is brought about by getting enough sleep and satisfying your bodily needs for rest, vitamins and minerals from foods, and sufficient exercise. These are all bodily needs.

The safety aspect of the chart relates to how safe you are in your home, how secure you feel with people that you know, and if you can mix socially with others without too much problem, then that part of the psyche is looked after. A woman who stays at home and mixes with no one isn't doing herself any favors, because she is introducing a lack of safety into her life. There's no one to care about her. There's no one to check in and see if she is okay, and that human contact forms part and parcel of the safety net that we put around our lives.

Love and belonging come next, and these are very important aspects of being happy. They start with the way that you feel about yourself and extend to the way that you feel about others, and how they feel about you. When you take care of your needs for love, you give, but you also allow yourself to take, so that this giving and taking is in equal proportions. You get joy from giving a friend a birthday gift or going to the movies with a friend, and you can share who you are with trusted people who trust you in return. The aspect here that affects people who have self-esteem issues is that they tend to put other peoples' needs before their own. If you are incomplete, how do you expect to attract complete and wholesome people into your tribe? The fact is that you need to be happy to spend time alone as well as being happy to share it, and self-love and appreciation come into this category. When you learn to love yourself, you open the doors to real love shown by others toward you. You make yourself worth loving. Is it worth loving someone who cannot love herself? You already know the answer to that one, so self-care is extremely important, and leaving yourself to last was never the right way to do things. Sometimes, you have to put other people's needs first, but certainly not as a general rule in life.

So how does esteem come into the picture? Well, this is all about what you think of yourself and the image that you portray to others. It is all about having the right boundaries and respecting the boundaries of others. When you have self-esteem, people know where they stand with you and are more likely to trust you as you show them that you trust yourself. Self-care allows you to show the world that you do care for yourself, and you can see many examples of this in a shopping mall simply by looking around you. The perceived emotional stature of people depends upon their comportment and the way that they interact with others, but also can be seen in the way that they look after themselves.

You can never be the best person you are capable of being when you don't look after yourself. Thus, the care that you give to yourself comes out in many ways. Now let's look at some of the different categories and see why they are so important to self-actualization.

The Food That You Eat

If you are always feeding yourself food that is not nourishing, your hair suffers, your skin suffers, and you are likely to gain weight. Weight gain will ultimately give you other health problems even if these are just digestive problems for the time being. Quite often, the way that you look after your body on the inside is reflected on the outside. People who eat too much grease, for example, may have skin problems and may even find that they are putting on weight in all the wrong places. If you make the most of eating and drinking the right things, you give your body a head start; your energy levels increase, and you feel healthier and happier.

The other important element of eating and drinking is taking in sufficient water, because the water within the body needs to be replenished. If you are always drinking coffee, it's a diuretic, which means that you will lose more water through your urine. Thus, drinking glasses of plain water regularly will help to make you feel wonderful. It helps your body to send that liquid refreshment to all the right parts of your body so that you don't suffer from cramps when you are overactive or underactive. Water really is an important part of the diet.

Allowing Yourself Enough Sleep

In this day and age, many women take their phones or tablets to bed and while away the time looking at their emails and updates on their Facebook pages. The problem with this at night is that you are not allowing your mind to switch off. Other things that can keep you awake at night are:

- A bedroom that is not sufficiently aired
- A bedroom with too much heat
- An uncomfortable mattress
- Sheets that are not fresh and welcoming
- A busy mind after watching action TV too late
- Worries from the day

You need to start thinking of your bedroom as a peaceful haven where sleep happens, and prepare yourself for sleep by relaxing a little after you switch off the TV. A good book may help, and leaving your technology out of the bedroom will do wonders for your eyesight. When you get into bed, try to relax. If you can't, and you are worried about things, try to meditate yourself to sleep. It works well, as does doing a body scan. This is where you breathe in the same way that you do when you meditate but concentrate on different areas of the body, starting with the toes and working your way up through all of your body parts. Focus on your toes; tense them, and then relax them, and see how good they feel relaxed in this manner. Move onto the next part of your body and do the same until your mind is sleepy, and you can get a good night's sleep.

The Way You Present Yourself to the World

This can have a lot to do with self-esteem and self-actualization. Take care of your skin by removing make-up at night. Make sure that your hair is regularly washed and treat yourself to a great conditioner now and again. If you have dyed hair, get it done regularly so that it doesn't look as if you don't care about your looks. Others always notice the way that you look after yourself. For example, if you don't clean your teeth regularly, you may have bad breath, or if you don't wash your face every day, perhaps you greet the world with sleepy eyes.

Look at yourself in the mirror often and especially when you are about to step out into the world. Check how you look. Approve of how you look because if you approve, then it's likely that the world is going to approve as well. Are you wearing clothes that are suited to the event? For example, your work clothes should show that you take care of yourself because they are a reflection of the company that you work for. If you want a managerial job, then you won't get it by not looking the part. Companies want their employees to show the world what the company standards are, so you must look your best for whatever job you do.

Similarly, working in a farm environment, you would hardly be welcome if you turned up in high heels and a short skirt. Practical jobs require practical clothing and reflect the thought that you put into what you are going to be doing. Dressing for a party is pretty safe if you check with the host(s) or other attendees as to what kind of dress is appropriate. These extra checks are worthwhile because when you know how you are expected to dress, you tend to look the part, rather than being unprepared and dressing inappropriately.

The Effect of Colors

You may not be aware of it, but if you dress in colors that are "happy" colors, you are likely to feel more optimistic toward the world, and if that helps your mental state, then it's worth trying when you are considering what to wear for the day.

Taking Care of Your Posture

In the old days, you would be encouraged by your parents to sit up straight. You would perhaps be encouraged to cross a room with a book on your head. The point of these exercises was to help you to grow strong and grow upright. The problems that you get from slouching can play on your mind, but they can also do more than that. They alter your body image to others. As you have learned about how to use posture when you are meditating, it's also a good idea to make sure that your body is comfortable rather than slouched as this can affect your health as well as the image you put forward to others.

The other element regarding your posture is the fact that you have energy centers throughout your spine, and if the energy flow is interrupted, you will find that you suffer as a consequence. It may be that you suffer aches and pains when you are worried about things, and a lot of this may be in the neck and shoulders area. Thus, it's vital to make sure that you keep this part of your body straight as much as you can. It will save you a lot of problems later.

What Self-Care Does to Your Esteem Levels

Throughout my work with women, I have found that self-care is the first step toward getting your self-esteem back. Looking after your body, confidently presenting yourself, and knowing that you are doing the best that you can for your health makes you feel good inside. You are much more likely to be loveable, but you are also more likely to love yourself when you practice ongoing care of the person that you have become. Nothing makes you feel greater than having a new hairstyle or managing a move in yoga that you never managed before, and the message that you are sending to your body is no longer one of neglect. It's telling the body to work as it's intended to work, with you in the driving seat.

Chapter Eight: Self-Love – 4 Paths to Self-Love

"You yourself, as much as anybody in the entire universe, deserve your love and affection" - Sharon Salzberg

Before I go further on this subject, I want you to understand something. No one on this earth has more control over the way that your life pans out than you. You may argue that you had a dreadful childhood. You may argue that you have been through some horrendous experiences in life, but so have millions of other women and there's nothing particularly special about any one of them except the way that they handled those situations and came out on the other side knowing that ultimately, they were responsible for their own happiness. Drop the concept that you need someone else because you are incomplete. You will always be incomplete if you think in this way. However, if you take time out and stop looking, you will find that all the strength that you need in your life is there inside you, and you just need to know how to access it.

Path One – Accepting the Now

I was once unfortunate enough to be at the bedside of a lady who was dying. All of her life, she carried the weight of her past with her. It didn't matter what you told her, she always came back to the past and never really started to see beyond that until it was too late, and she was filled with regret at all of the years she had wasted in retrospection. I don't want that to happen to anyone who reads this book, and if I have anything to do with it, you won't need to go there. The first step toward self-love is accepting yourself at this moment in time, and although it sounds simple, many people in this world refuse to do that and carry on having self-esteem issues, when it's so easy to step into this moment and tell yourself that you are not a product of anything that anyone else has done to you, or of the sins that have happened in your past. You are now, and every moment of your life counts. Start to pull yourself back into this moment because that's all there is, and it can be a moment filled with misery or it can be a moment filled with the joy of being alive. Look at nature to help you. Be inspired by it. Watch the spider as he makes his web, or the flowers pop their heads up in spring to let you know that another year lies ahead. Be aware of the world around you and your part in it because that's where happiness lies, and that's where self-esteem starts.

Path Two: Believing in What You Want Out of Your Life

I talk to a lot of people about what they want, and instead of looking inside themselves for true wishes and dreams, they tend to look at material things. They also have a little voice inside them that tells them that they are never going to achieve their dreams, and this is self-defeating. You have to draw up a plan of what you want in your life, and instead of telling yourself that you can't have it, tell yourself that you already have it but that it's simply not accessible at this moment. You have to change the mindset because if you work against yourself, you are never going to love who you are. See yourself as confident and happy, and let that happiness happen. See yourself as wanting to live in a big house and keep on believing that it will happen because the moment you stop believing, you cut off your dreams and start to become very unhappy about who you are, and that's not fair to your inner self. Let yourself dream. Let your dreams be as specific as possible and believe wholeheartedly in them. It gives you a personal stand upon which to feel that you deserve the life you crave, and indeed you do, and it's only by not loving who you are that you stand back and watch others succeed and see yourself fail because you don't believe you deserve a life like theirs. You do. Everyone does.

Path Three: Acceptance

When you are a kid, it's hard to accept that the neighbor's kid has a new bike and you don't. As you grow older, you find that life isn't as simplistic as that. Perhaps the kids who had "everything" didn't actually have much. Their parents were too busy working to provide them with material things so that when it came to love and family, they weren't around much. There are always two ways of looking at everything, and when you accept who you are and where you are in life, you get to realize life is a one-way street. You are not practicing; this isn't a dry run that you can waste on self-indulgence being unhappy about who you have become. However, when you accept who you are, you find happiness within yourself that helps you to love and respect yourself for who you are. You are attracted to people who accept themselves and make good friendships that last a lifetime. Why? Because people who think like this don't look for all the regrets in their lives. They are too busy living in the moment and enjoying it.

Path Four: Use Your Losses to Become Emotionally Stronger

When you feel that you will crumble at the end of a bad relationship, the truth of the matter is that you won't crumble. You may feel bad, but you make yourself feel a whole lot worse if you throw blame into the equation. Self-blame, the blame for your partner, these are all excuses not to move on. When Kelly was told that her husband, Mark, had been killed in action, her world stopped turning for a short while, but as she stood beside his grave, looking on as the coffin was lowered into the ground, she felt a swell of love inside her that she hadn't noticed before. He had loved her. They had completed years and years of marriage and had a child that would grow up and become someone her father would be proud of. Yes, there was the anger, the regret, the unhappiness of loss, and the natural grief process, but what woke Kelly up was the fact that every day of her life with Mark, he had made her feel like she deserved life, and she did. She worked hard, she made a small humble house into a home, and these had been the best years of her life so far. What she needed to do was continue to be emotionally strong and happy inside her heart, so she used the loss as a steppingstone that helped her to help others – not because she wanted any kind of status, but simply because she could. She had learned through loss to be more compassionate in life, to be humble, and to give whatever she could to the moment that she was in. She also saw other people who, like her, had lost partners but who were not coping as well as she was, and she helped them to rebuild their lives.

No matter how badly off you are or how you believe that life has mistreated you up until this moment in time, those lessons should be clues as to how to make your life count for more than the hurt other people foisted on you; you are not a victim. You might have been in the past, but as long as you carry the victim mentality with you, you will remain one when in fact you can step out of that shell any time that you want to and use those experiences of your life to let others know that it's okay to have bad experiences, as long as you can get to the other side of them with self-love intact. Kelly started to work with other people who were feeling the same needs as hers, and through that work realized that she was worthy of the love that Mark had given her during his life, and in loving herself honored his memory in her own way.

Step Five: Forgive Others and Forgive Yourself

You are a human being, and regardless of your religion, agnosticism, or atheism, you should have learned by now that mankind is not perfect. Mistakes get made, and so many people use blame as an excuse not to move on. If you blame yourself for your misfortunes in life, you never actually get past them because you see yourself as defective. That self-image goes with you for the rest of your life unless you are prepared to forgive and forget. If you blame yourself for something, move on; forgive yourself, because forgiveness heals the scars and helps you to start over without always thinking negative thoughts about who you are. If you have had problems forgiving others, let go. It doesn't take a lot of imagination to see what this hatred or what this blame does to you; it makes you bitter. It cuts into who you are and takes away your self-esteem. Angry people don't like themselves much, so let go of the anger. Write a letter if you want to forgive someone; let them know it's all in the past and that you have moved on. If you are too nervous about sending it, just accept that you have forgiven and let go of the past for good. When you can do this, you become a whole person and can love yourself again. You can't love someone who is always blaming others or blaming self, because it's self-defeating.

In the next chapter, I am going to cover goals, because goals help you to love yourself too, but they do need explaining in full, so I am not going to use that in this chapter on self-love. Try to remember what you felt like as a child when you received something that made you feel wonderful inside, or when you saw something that filled you with wonder. Then close your eyes for a moment. You are an incredible human being. Whether you are a believer in a higher power or not, your human body is that of a goddess. It sustains you. It allows you to do so much in your life. You can see, hear, smell, taste, touch, and even sense things in the world around you. Isn't that incredible? What's not to love about something that works in harmony with nature, and that offers you all of these rewards?

All that you need to do to regain self-love is to appreciate who you are. Be thankful when you wake up in the morning and think of all of the things that you are grateful for, as that helps reinforce how wonderful the gift of life is. You were given this gift, and if you can't love it and look after it, then you cannot expect it to know what to do when times get tough. However, if you love it and care for it, it's there to make you a very strong person when life is tough, and to take your hand as you cross the steppingstones of life. You may not know it, but life is what moves you from one steppingstone to the next. Think of it as an invisible friend inside you, giving you strength and love, and when you think of yourself in this way, you can't deny that person that you are the love that you deserve. Self-love has nothing to do with vanity. It has nothing to do with what you own. It has nothing to do with comparisons. It's all about accepting the gift of life and treasuring it.

Chapter Nine: Setting Goals

"If you want to live a happy life, tie it to a goal, not to people or things." - Albert Einstein

What does this have to do with self-esteem? Ask yourself how you feel when you achieve something; even if that achievement is relatively small, you feel good about it because you did it. That's why goals help you to increase your self-esteem. The first time that you do something and finish it, you feel like someone has switched on the light, and it's great to feel capable. This all works toward being a better you, and it also means that you are more accomplished than you were before you did that thing. A child learns all about the world through achievements. The first time a child walks, parents celebrate it. The first time a school kid ties his own laces, that's an achievement that makes the child feel a little less dependent upon adults to do things for him. It continues throughout your life as you accumulate knowledge, but you also need to set yourself small goals if you want your life to go in a forward direction.

When you know what you want in your life, your core goals help you to get there. For example, if you want to travel the world, that first $10 put away in a savings account is a step in the right direction. If you want to become a doctor, aiming at taking the necessary examinations is a stepping stone toward success; all of the things you want to do in life are potentials, and the goals that you make should align with what you want to do. You want to be happier in your life; then, the goal is to meditate daily to help you to become happier in yourself. If you want to live in a nice home, then a goal of decluttering will help you. The goals that take you there don't have to be huge; getting rid of one single bit of clutter is a goal that is taking you in the right direction.

The problem that people with low self-esteem have is that they see the goals in their lives as insurmountable. No goal is insurmountable; it can be broken down into very small tasks that lead you in the direction you want to go. Nothing is beyond the scope of possibility if you start to make small, doable goals. So how do you start with goals if you feel that your self-esteem is low? You decide tonight what you want to do tomorrow. If you can't manage to plan for the whole day, plan for the morning. Then at lunch, make another plan for the afternoon. Goals begin with thinking and then are listed so that you have guidelines of what you are supposed to do. They come in different types too:

- Short term goals – What will you do tonight or tomorrow?
- Medium-term goals – What do you want to achieve this week?
- Long term goals – What dreams do you have for the future?

I would suggest that you start with small goals, and as you gain confidence, start to plan medium-term goals, and then eventually, it will come naturally that long term goals help you to steer your life in the direction you want it to go. It helps your self-esteem and helps you to respect who you are if you set goals and then get to cross them out as you achieve them, but beware; if you get over-ambitious and set impossible goals, you set yourself up for failure, which is why I say that you should start your goal-setting with small things that you can easily manage and then work toward goals that are a little harder.

There are no excuses for not reaching your goals. For example, if you don't do all of the things you have on your list, then the reason is that you set your expectations too high and should start with smaller goals. It's no one's fault. It's just that you have not become accustomed to goalkeeping, so don't beat yourself up if you fail on the first couple of attempts. The idea is always to be realistic in your goals. For example, these could include things that seem relatively mundane, but when you add all of the small achievements together, they all make you feel better about yourself. Here are a few examples that you can use, or you can make goals that are more relevant to your particular case:

- I will clean my shoes tomorrow
- I will leave the kitchen clean after breakfast
- I will set my clothes out tonight for tomorrow
- I will go to bed at ten o'clock tonight
- I will eat more vegetables today
- I will cut out the snacks this morning
- I will smoke less this morning

These may not appear to be much to do, but I don't know the level of your self-esteem, so it's important to start with basic goals before you work your way to more serious goals. The above goals are simply to demonstrate the kind of things that you can use as your goals. Perhaps you neglect yourself, and your goals could include:

- I will wash my hair today
- I will make sure to apply my skin cream
- I will wear make-up today

You make the rules, but when you achieve a goal, you use a big red pen to strike those items off your list that you have achieved. The idea is to try to strike off all of the items on the list that you have made for yourself. If you give priority to these tasks, you will find that you achieve them when you don't allow the interruptions of life get in the way.

As far as work goes, perhaps some goals will help you to achieve more. For example, if you use a system whereby you work without any interruption for a set amount of time in the morning, you achieve more. Hence, turn off telephones or put them onto voicemail. Don't look at your cell phone and certainly do not think of looking at social media during this time. Give yourself a goal of one hour of concentrated work; it's great to stand up and have a break halfway through, and then go back to that concentrated work on the more complex items that you have to do. The reason these goals are great in the morning is that after your meditation, your mind is refreshed and has its highest energy levels, so difficult tasks are easier to perform.

You may want to have a goal about the way that you interact with other people within the work environment. Many people are unhappy at work and don't interact in a friendly way with others. A smile at someone can go a very long way, so make this a goal. Perhaps you see someone struggling with their workload and can help out. Make helpfulness a daily goal, and no matter how small your helpfulness is, it counts. For example, getting your boss a cup of coffee is kind, but so is helping a colleague with a problem. Make a goal of including two acts of kindness within your day and feel good when you achieve that. You can even stretch this to more acts of kindness at a later date, and this will help your self-esteem levels.

The goals that you set long term should include making your dreams come true. If you want to do something that costs money, then look at savings you can make on things that don't matter that much to you. You will have more money in the long term by deciding to cut down on something today. Perhaps you don't even enjoy your TV much. Limit viewing and save electricity, and free up time to do something more constructive. Perhaps you don't need to pay for all those extra channels you don't even watch. What about your phone contract? Do you need to pay as much as you are? When you have long term goals, you tend to think more in terms of economic adjustments you can make to get to the long-term goals more easily. Goals help your self-esteem, but they also help you to find some sense in your life and reasons for doing what you do.

If you find that you have neglected valuable friendships, you could make a goal to telephone or visit that friend, and at the same time, reinforce the friendship, which is also good for your self-esteem. If you have a free weekend, why not help out at a local dog shelter? This kind of activity may not fit with your long-term goals, but it's great for your self-esteem and helps you to feel that your life is purposeful. There are so many goals that you can set, and you can even split these into different categories such as:

- Relationship goals
- Work goals
- Personal development goals

Relationship goals are important because one phone call can make a world of difference in the way that you feel, and being in touch with positive people will also help your self-esteem. Relationship goals can even include your relationship with yourself because you have to be happy with that before you can work on more serious goals that involve others.

Work goals mean going out of your way to prove your worth, even if only to yourself. Whatever you are capable of within the workplace, make it a priority to do the best that you can during working hours, so that you maximize your opportunities to be relied upon and for promotion. Let everyone know your worth simply by doing the job right, and you don't need anyone's validation. Your goals will tell you how well you are doing, and you can always up the ante when the goals are too easy to achieve.

Personal development goals:

- Looking your best
- Optimizing the way that you present yourself to the world
- Learning something new so that you don't stagnate
- Doing something each day that is pure pleasure for you

There are so many things that people want to include in their lives, but they find that there isn't time to do those things. You have to make small goals that lead you to open up your full potential. For example, why not listen to a language course while commuting to work? What about stopping by the gym on the way home? How about reading the book you have been promising you will read and giving yourself some downtime to do things that make a great difference to your life? Learning is always going to make you feel more valuable because the knowledge that you gain during your life is so useful to you. It can also give you a real sense of achievement.

No matter how small your goals are when you start to use goals for personal development, they are helping you to move toward bigger and better goals, but the biggest boost you get from goal-achieving is that you can actually see yourself improving and get a real buzz out of striking those goals off your list.

You are a wonderful human being but have perhaps inherited goals that do not suit you. These are your choices from now on. Walk with faith in your heart that you can make goals and keep them so that you become an achiever, and with that achievement, become self-assured and self-confident. The purpose of a goal is to give you a direction to your life, and no matter how small those goals may be, a sense of direction gets you there faster.

For the time being, sit down with your notepad and write down the goals for tomorrow morning. Try to achieve them. Don't be too ambitious. If you are not already a goal-oriented woman, it will take time to get there, but little goals and achievements will enthuse you sufficiently to make bigger goals and to experience bigger achievements.

Remember not to weigh yourself down with so many goals that you cannot possibly achieve them. A few for tomorrow morning will lead to a few for tomorrow afternoon. As you make this habit stick, you will find that your goals become your rewards and that your life takes on a new meaning and order, where all things become possible. Do not limit yourself by setting out on a journey without knowing where you are heading.

Conclusion

"*The very least you can do in your life is to figure out what you hope for. And the most you can do is live inside that hope. Not admire it from a distance but live right in it, under its roof.*" - Barbara Kingsolver

Now that you have read through the chapters of this book, that doesn't mean the work is finished. It is only just beginning. The tools that you will need to make all of this work are the following:

- A notebook – to write down your progress, to keep notes and to list goals
- A red marker – to cross off your goals as you achieve them
- A meditation space – to give you the peace of mind you need to move forward

I would also ask that you go back through the chapters and take notes of those areas that affect you or that you feel will help you to develop your self-esteem. It is easy to look backward in life and regret things that have happened. It's far harder to forgive and move on, but when you take the route that is suggested in this book, you will find you are not alone. There are thousands of women out there in the world with whom you can share what you learn. Not only will this help your self-esteem, but it will also give you purpose and a very good reason to continue the habits that are outlined in Chapter Six. However, before you get there, the idea of Chapter Four was to introduce you to yourself, and that's an extremely important part of fixing your self-esteem because the physiological working of the human body may be what is holding you back. The care that you give to your body counts when it comes to feeding the body with all of the fuel it needs to present you to the world as a complete and happy human being.

You have learned the part that the brain plays in self-esteem, and that's an important lesson. Don't hesitate to go back to the chapters to reinforce your values and to ensure that you stick to the suggested habits. You are more in control of things than you give yourself credit for. Although parts of the book relate to anxiety and fears, knowing how your body works helps you to understand the reactions that you live with every day of your life. Those fears could be controllable as could the anxiety, just by knowing what's going on inside you and why you feel that momentary panic in the first place.

I want you to shine. I want you to be able to move on from reading this book to a better understanding of life because, at the end of the day, your life counts from the moment you decide to make it count. Start to plan your journey. Start to realize what your long-term ambitions are and make your life head in the right direction.

The most important aspect of all of this is that you are now living in the moment. What happened to you in the past only remains a part of you for as long as you allow it to. Now is the time to forgive and move on so that the events of the past do not dictate your level of self-esteem today. Think of self-esteem as the way that you look at yourself, and when you start to respect yourself and see good things, then you will find that those around you respect that Goddess that you may have kept hidden until now.

There is a lot of reference material within the book, and it's worthwhile following the links to the suggested YouTube videos as these are an important part of reinforcing what was said within the pages of the book. Learning to care for yourself is part of the journey; if you stop along the way to enjoy a sunset or to eat an ice-cream, then good for you! It is spontaneous acts of joy that make your world a better place and inspire you to carry on positively.

I am happy that you read the book cover to cover and that you have arrived here, at the end of the book, but at the beginning of a new understanding of who you are as a woman, and that you can now go forward with the guidance of the book. Self-esteem and confidence are worked on for the simple reason that life chips away at them, and although some women already know the remedy to fight back, others are not as aware of what helps to mend those chinks in their armor. Now you are, and I hope that you move forward, proud of what you learned and able to live the life that you fully deserve.

Check out another book by Dara Montano

www.ingramcontent.com/pod-product-compliance
Lightning Source LLC
Chambersburg PA
CBHW070046230426
43661CB00005B/782